Copyright © "Harrisons Angel" 2024

The right of "Harrisons Angel" to be identified as the author of this work has been asserted by her in accordance with the Copyright, Designs and Patents Act 1988.

All rights reserved. No part of this publication may be reproduced, stored in a retrieval system, or transmitted, in any form or by any means without the prior written permission of the author, nor be otherwise circulated, in any form of binding or cover other than which it has been designed and printed initially by "Harrisons Angel".

ISBN: 9798334766419

As my ancient computer is not compatible with anything other than the basic ancient version of word, sadly there are no page numbers. After endlessly fretting about this I have decided that it has to be considered a "non-problem" in the grander scheme of things. The book is a little different, so it's format may as well be too!

Four years ago I was told that this book would be a best seller. As of yet I have sold one copy to my bestmate!

If one day what I was told finally comes true, this copy would be priceless.

Even if it doesnt this book is priceless to me + who told me to write it :)

Love
Harrisons Angel XXX
9/11/2025

Dedicated to all of the beautiful souls I love.

And especially for Bill, Dopey, Olivia, Dhani and Little George The Positive Potato.

XXX

I Have a Dream

"The Calling"

By

Harrisons Angel

SOMETHING "OUT THERE" THAT IS FAR BIGGER THAN US...

A Starting Point...

We must look beyond ourselves for us to be able to stay connected with our fellow man. We need to look closely at the people around us, and notice the sad, lonely and the poor. Because if we lose our ability to look beyond ourselves, we lose our compassion. And there becomes no gauge or thermometer to assess ourselves or others accurately by. In a world that is currently steeped in self-professed victimhood. Try and remember that there will always be someone out there in the world who has suffered more than you. That in its self is motivation to try and move past any hurt within, for they may not be able to.

There is so much beauty in our world, but yet many have become blinded by technology and the need to self-soothe by any means at their disposal. Quick fixes that we all need at times, and of course we must enjoy life, but balance is the key. Voids within us cannot be filled solely by material items and distractions alone. There is something "out there" that can help us all on our life journey. It is free and will sustain us when we are lacking. It does not need to impress us; it is universal and does not need algorithms to appeal to our preferences. Once we have it in our sights it is a permanent unchanging feature, which will keep us focused in a world that is becoming lost within human ego's.

I want you to see it, and the world needs us all to see it. But to do so, you have to be open to the possibility that logic plays no part in the big reveal. Belief and love is all you need, and then I am sure you will experience all that you need to clarify its existence. You may need a small nudge in the right direction, but it's not the journey but the destination that matters.

PLAY: CONTRACT NUMBER 77777

If by Rudyard Kipling is my "go to" poem, if you can relate to the words, and you have earned the seen it, been there and done that tee shirt. But remain determined to never give up and only have had brief stays at The Pity Party Plaza. Which is located on the same dark desert highway as Hotel California and Heartbreak Hotel, we are on precisely the same page. But if life has left you feeling world weary, and you are a regular guest at one of these hotels. Please don't believe any of the night staff who may tell you that you can never leave, you can check out any time when you feel ready. And I am more than happy to arrange all that is necessary for your escape, and after wiping your feet on departure you will receive an automatic and free upgrade to Self-Acceptance Manor which is located on the Sunny Side of the street. And for those of you who may feel lost and homeless because life has thrown far too much your way. Please reach out for my extended hand and trust me when I tell you that you are not alone...

A beautiful and peaceful home from home awaits you that welcomes rather than imprisons its guests and has limitless rooms for all souls who wish to stay. I have met many of you already in the beautiful foyer which has wallpaper to die for, and the most wonderful bespoke hand-crafted display cabinets. On arrival, please inspect them closely as you will find an exact replica of your most precious and treasured keepsake. Which will remain on display for eternity and be a permanent reminder of all your greatest achievements.

I am a volunteer at the Manor and undertake many tasks, however this is the first time I have conducted a tour. For approximately six hours, I will escort you around some of this beautiful building's private rooms, which are normally off limits to members of the public, and I will also show you the Manors very secret garden and private beach. Many of the rooms have recently been decorated whilst others have remained untouched for almost sixty years. The tours itinerary may seem a little paradoxical at times, but it is essential that you see the entire building and grounds to get a feel for it. A team of interior designers have all been allocated one of the untouched rooms and have each been given a budget of £3000 to conduct a makeover, which will commence as soon as the room is vacant.

The final stop of the tour will be my room which is simply decorated with whitewashed walls and a solid wood parquetry floor. One wall has a huge multi-coloured stained-glass window depicting all that I consider to be spiritual and peaceful; Jesus, angels, flowers, butterflies, the absolute works. Positioned in the centre of the room is the largest snuggle (Lemsip advert style) chair imaginable, with high sides and back which is in the most beautiful shade of cobalt blue. It has far too many gorgeous jewel-coloured cushions and I am often found sitting there. I may be reading, listening to beautiful music, praying, watching telly, drinking a glass of chardonnay, eating a mini quiche, contemplating my navel or singing, which I am absolutely terrible at. But I can do mean impressions of Kate Bush singing Wuthering Heights and Eliza Doolittle's rendition of Wouldn't it be Luverly from My Fair Lady. You could well catch me dancing around on the wooden floor with not a care in the world. But equally you may also find me in tears of frustration and sadness as I struggle to make sense of this world. Feeling increasingly impotent that my single pair of hands and silenced voice is unable to help people who are in desperate need. I am not a polarized and singular narrative and who can say what I will be doing on any given day, and I am in no doubt that I will surprise you.

Whilst we spend our last moments together in my sanctuary and before you retire to yours, which I promise you will adore. It would be wonderful if we could all have a group hug and make three wishes. Wishes made amongst the warmest of hugs, that we will then pass onto those who for various reasons were unable to join us on our tour. The Trivago star rating for the Manor is limitless and the more recommendations this place gets the brighter its well-earned stars will shine. And with a little luck one day they may illuminate the very darkest of places.

Why The Manor Requested I Conduct This Tour

I am a Myers Briggs INFJ which is also known as The Advocate and is the rarest of the 16 personality types and encompasses 2% of the population. The Myers Briggs test was constructed by Katherine Cook Briggs and her daughter Isabel Briggs Myers who were inspired by the book Psychological Types by Swiss psychiatrist Carl Jung.

Famous INFJ's include Jesus, George Harrison, Martin Luther King Junior, Eleanor Roosevelt, Mahatma Gandhi, Carl Jung, Morgan Freeman, Derren Brown, Jane Goodall, Peter Gabriel, Alanis Morrisette, Taylor Swift and JK Rowling.

Without knowing anything about the Myers Briggs Test, these words may spring to mind when describing this varied group of people: Passionate, possibly introverted, artistic, altruistic and unusual. Traits that can be attributed to their actions and general demeanour. Of course there is far more to all of these people, and with the exception of Jesus INFJ's are far from perfect. We are just as flawed as every other human being. But as a rule of thumb, we are empathetic and incredibly passionate about the world, and are egalitarians who will try and use their positive traits for the greater good. We are not afraid to walk alone and will happily run through the herd to a lone destination rather than follow others blindly.

Often from an early age INFJ's feel that they have a task to complete whilst they are alive. Whether it is to spread Gods word, write and perform songs that reach out to the masses, protect chimpanzees, or make others think about how they or the generic mind perceives and interprets information. They will usually achieve their goal and leave their positive mark on the world, because they are passionate and determined. Particularly when the task feels like a contractual agreement that has been signed in indelible ink, possibly even before they were born.

Whether this contractual agreement is an internal message and solely to do with the makeup of an individual's brain, or something "out there" has set the task, who can say. I cannot speak for others but for me it has always felt like an external influence. I signed my contract many years ago when I heard a very beautiful song and had a photograph taken of me at around the same time. My spiritual or INFJ "to do" was never actioned because I had no clue as to what my task was. Occasionally I would come across the photo of me and these words always came into my mind "One day I will be looking back at people you do not know". I didn't understand how this could ever happen and for what reason.

To my surprise many years later in 2020 my task was finally revealed to me. The little photo finally uttered the words and enlightened me. I had to write a book and she would be on the back cover. My rare personality type and life experiences, many of which were current "hot topics" would work in unison to achieve three very specific goals, which could not have been any closer to my heart. I knew immediately that it must have a word count of 77,777 which relates to one of the books main goals. And as I often think in lyrics, I thought that it would be a wonderful idea to marry up my favourite songs with my personal experiences and INFJ thoughts on the world. It was going to be a concept rather than a memoir, and I was as certain as I could be that it was unique. And so, on October 1st of that year I began my task, and I completed my part of the contract in ten days, or at least I thought I had!

Sonia from PDF was my freebie editor, and she spoke my words back to me in her "Natural English" voice like the pro she is. She spoke as if she is talking to a dear friend with absolutely no airs and graces. I suspect at times I may come across as common as muck, but I know that true friends accept you as you are, and most familiar conversations are not in the least bit contrived. It is often the case that the simplest things in life mean so much more than grandiose gestures relating to displays of love or intelligence. When you take the padding away, there is not always true sentiment behind professed love, or emotional intelligence to back up academic brilliance. There is nothing wrong with ordinary, basic and simple if there is true sentiment behind any action.

When I had finished it, I dreamt of a lottery win and how the book could be distributed, Banksy style. My plan was to employ a group of dancers who would wear bear costumes and perform Flashdance around the entire Country, during the routine the free book would be given out to all who were in the vicinity. I would have paid no active part in its promotion and the little bears wonderful routine would be more than sufficient to draw attention to the book. A beautiful but unrealistic pipe dream that I had to swiftly move on from and accept that my only option to try and get my words out there was with a literary agents help.

As an introvert who prefers to sit at the back of a room and observe. And who avoids drawing attention to themselves for fear of looking a first class plonker, the very prospect filled me with dread.

And so began the submission process...

And much to my dismay it soon became apparent that even if it had been well written, it was never going to be published for two reasons. The first reason will be explained within the book's pages. And the second was that it was nigh on impossible trying to explain to an agent in a word restricted cover letter, synopsis and a couple of sample chapters why the book was relevant, current and different. I knew that the only way the messages within the pages could be imparted, was if the book was read in its entirety. Which is not permitted unless an agent requests the full manuscript after reading your initial submission.

And so, I had no option but to adapt the cover letter to fit agents very specific wish lists, to try and ignite the tiniest spark of interest. I also had to down play the books purpose and the reason why it had been written But by doing so this lessened the very message I needed to impart. I was self censoring, and it broke my heart that I had no option but to do so. I am naturally polite and try and always say something positive to make a person feel good about themselves. But the cover letter guidelines and criteria often involved a direct order to massage the agent's egos, whilst aligning directly with their values and interests. A few I genuinely could relate to, and I was being entirely honest with them, whilst others I had absolutely nothing in common with. But I had to play the game. I felt inauthentic, uncomfortable and truthfully a little tainted by the entire process. Even if I had been an accomplished and successful writer, I would have felt precisely the same about the entire dynamic.

A couple of years later I put a version onto Amazon, and designed some leaflets and did a boot sale to pay for them. Which I then delivered often in the pouring rain. Whilst doing so several people approached me and spoke to me and began to tell me their opinions on life. They told me that the book was a really good concept and one which they completely understood. I was sure I would get a couple of eBook sales but nothing, a big fat very much in your face zero. I knew the book was far from perfect but as an avid reader I had read far worse. It felt like I was being pushed forward and then a giant hand would stop me and let me have a breather. And then like a little clockwork toy it would wind me up again release me and send me down a different path, only to be stopped yet again.

Not one living soul who knew I had written it understood why I had done so. They clearly thought I was having a mid- life crisis and if they had made a disingenuous remark, I would have noticed, and so they all stayed stum.

My logical brain was screaming at me to stop, this is not going to happen, the book is far too left field. Just because you know that there is a market for a book written by a Christian, INFJ, working-class, middle-aged woman the world you live in knows otherwise. You have no social media presence to aid book sales, Joanna Bloggs crawl back into your hermit shell. And just for the record although you are pretty good at Business English. Writing in first person is best left to the professionals. You are absolutely rubbish at punctuation, and you sometimes write where instead of were. Seriously, do yourself a favour and knock it on the head. Go and do something far more productive, like finishing your diamond art picture. No one wants an egalitarian hug, and why on earth would they, when there are Facebook likes a plenty. Listen to the naysayers and doubters they are spot on; you are wasting your time.... Loser.

Logic won this internal battle, I listened and stopped. Finally finished my diamond art picture and started another. And then something nudged me to try once more and so I did. And after yet another round of failed submissions I felt like a participant in the old show Candid Camera, who was on the receiving end of a never-ending spiritual wind-up.

And so, I decided to take another break for a few months, and reflect on how I was feeling about the book and myself. It was not a matter of pride or determination to succeed, I felt like a vessel that was being guided and pushed in a certain direction and I had absolutely no option but to comply. When I looked at the book with fresh eyes, it was as if the once passionately written pages had been covered by a thin veil which had been removed. My enthusiasm for the book was re-ignited, and I worked on it once again until I felt satisfied. I had learnt a valuable lesson, and one that I shall never forget. Now that the book is once more a true reflection of me, I feel more peaceful than I ever have.

I choose to remain anonymous firstly because I knew it was the right course of action. I believe that a lot of the world's problems are due to many human beings' egos being out of control. I consider myself just a soul encased in an earthly suit and my name is not relevant. And secondly for my family, some of whom are written about in glowing terms and others are not, regardless of their roles within the book I remain protective of them. And finally, as an atypical INFJ I am incredibly private and introverted by nature. I have never courted or desired attention, and I do not understand those who excessively do so.

Throughout the tour I shall refer to myself as Kim, which is a nod to the book Kim by Rudyard Kipling. And, because I like short and to the point, I cannot stand unnecessary padding with regards to words whether written or spoken. Just as the very funny comedy duo Trevor and Simon didn't do duvets, I don't normally do padding.

I remain certain that I was assigned this task, a calling if you will. And over the past four years I have moved further along my spiritual path. Each and every event and experience was meant to happen. Some have been incredibly painful but all have enlightened me. It has been an organic process and the books contents have changed and evolved just as much as I have, and all for the better. I have learnt a few life lessons and have changed my opinion on several different matters. It has been a journey of discovery and my faith has been put to the test, but not once have I lost it. It has not been an easy path to walk but it is one that I am blessed to have trod. And what does not kill us, truly does make us stronger.

This task by the way could have been assigned to absolutely anyone, I am not remotely special, but I am incredibly determined. You will soon discover that I represent all of us ordinary folks, who have often been put down by others and bullied. Subsequently this has led many of us to feel racked with self-doubt and this has rendered us silent. Voices that are often right but are never listened to, not until it is too late. It breaks my heart to say that we are coming very close to this point, and if we don't peacefully speak out now this window of opportunity will be lost.

Being dismissed as crazy is the norm to me, even when I have always spoken the truth, and I expect no different with regards to this calling. I can imagine people saying Why her? Many of her family have mental health issues, she is deluded, she has had a psychotic episode, she is nuts. I admit to being extremely ordinary but I am not crazy. I would be lying if I said that I was happy about being set a task that I suspect no one is going to believe. But yet there have been stories about people who claim to have had very long chats with God, which people believe and they have been best sellers. If I had simply been told to write a book about narcissism to help others then I could have got my head round this. But to be essentially told that it must have repeated sevens as a word count, a number which is used throughout the bible, is a very big deal.

This was never about money or recognition; in fact, it was always the reverse. I had no option but to do as I was told and I trust that God will provide for me whilst I am down here. Whatever will be will be, and even if my words remain hidden, and this was simply a task that I had to complete to show my true heart to my Father in Heaven, then all is good and precisely as it should be. And when my earthly shift comes to an end, I will request that this odd little unplanned book will be placed in my casket with me, and we will leave this world at peace and be at one together.

So, let's get this party started as in Shirley Bassey, and have a fab time, but let's also share our sad moments too. A life journey with many different stops: faith, love, life, loss and all manner of things in-between.

It's time to take you away ....

Poem: God's Hall of Fame by Alf Hutchison

Songs/Music My Sweet Lord by George Harrison (Dhani's latest "Out There" version)

Greensleeves best version diemauerdk (beautiful graphics)

With regards to the poems and songs mentioned none of the lyrics or words are written down and this adheres to copyright law. It would be wonderful if you could pause reading and press play on YouTube whenever they appear. It's all part of the package deal :) xxx

ROOM 1

The Unscheduled Detour

As I realize the importance of words whether spoken or written I know without a shadow of a doubt that if I manage to complete this, it will be checked and edited a million times. I am the person whose blood runs cold when predictive text interferes with my much thought-out message. Have I got the tone right and will it convey what is necessary, could it be misconstrued? A million scenarios run through my mind, and none of them remotely matter to anyone but me. God help anyone who has initiated contact and are waiting for an immediate response, I need at least ten minutes to gather myself or longer if I am mid Wordle or watching The Great Pottery Throwdown. The pressure is far too much, will it be possible for me to imbue a sense of calm and serenity particularly when I may have had an appalling day. So, I wait before responding, I mentally plan my reply, write a little, ponder, check, put myself in their shoes for a minute or so (unless they are a complete arse) and edit if necessary. Nearly there tone right...check, not too much padding... check, does it make the recipient feel valued and listened to... check, no apparent typos...check. Repeat process so no stone has been left unturned.... it's ready and so with the tiniest amount of very unhealthy trepidation I press send.

Mission accomplished, I perform one final check before I can return to my Wordle or can cry in unison with the lovely Keith Brymer Jones. My breathing rate returns to normal, and then suddenly there is a predictive text error which seems to have jumped from the screen and has formed into a CGI image. A little biplane is performing aerobatics in far too close proximity to my eyes, and is towing a banner which displays the error in neon shouty capitals. OMG how can I ever live this down, this person will think I can't spell, an immediate response is warranted... "Sorry I meant meet not meat" with added wacky face emoji to denote full ownership of eccentricity which is far preferable to dumb arse! Yes, a little mistake like that will freak me out, but I am relaxed about most things in fact I am pretty laid back, apart from being a cushion plumper and straightener before I hit the sack.

I am truly blessed with my lot and have so much to be very grateful for. And I have experienced many things throughout my life some would be considered bog standard but many are not. I wouldn't change a single thing and I believe that all that I have experienced was meant to be. As well as my faith music has also helped me throughout my life. It has comforted me like the warmest of hugs and has also been my port in many storms. I love dancing too particularly to old school trance, and I am still able to throw some very dubious shapes. Albeit with the added bonus of an arthritic clicking musical accompaniment.

However, my current and rather lame kitchen routines are unremarkable in comparison to my legendary performance of Flash Dance. Which was performed one Saturday afternoon over thirty years ago to entertain my bored toddler daughter. It was extremely intense, and I had very nearly worked up a sweat after frantically running on the spot with her for far longer than was necessary. We then decided to go solo, and she strutted her stuff wagging her finger and pointing at each of the invisible judges. Whilst I decided to freestyle and introduce the iconic star jump from Fame. The local taxis were all out on jobs, so I opted for the two-seater settee as my launch pad. I went for it big time and managed to get my legs a satisfactory three feet apart, and promptly landed like a sack of potatoes, which my daughter found hilarious. Nothing that an ice pack and crepe bandage couldn't sort out, and it was worth every single minute of fun. But never to be repeated, the routine is best left to the true experts.

I am very grateful to a lady called Celeste, for albeit unintentionally being the catalyst that nudged me into putting my fingers onto this keyboard. She frequently told me that her dream was to write a book but had no clue what to write about or how to start the dreaded first page. A turquoise retro typewriter which had belonged to an author whose work had been published, will remain idle in her beautiful colour coordinated office. Whilst I am on the starting blocks on my ancient computer, which is hardly used. What's the point when my Nokia can get me on Ebay? And if I need a bigger screen to research something, my £49 Amazon Tablet is more than adequate.

Seriously if this computer can last out for this book attempt it will be because of an ethereal intervention courtesy of Angels Brabentia and Rowenta , who have more powers than their aging colleagues Hoover and Whirlpool. The big guns are needed to keep this obsolete computer running, particularly as it is in the hands of an absolute computer phobic, middle-aged luddite.

Celeste is not her real name, which I am sure you have gathered already. Celeste is a frequent pop up that appears on all manner of internet searches, for no apparent reason. She has long silver hair and an enticing engaging half smile which beckons you to enter her ethereal realm to have a free angel reading. Which of course is decidedly dodgy for all manner of reasons. The main being on entering all of your details it is highly likely that you will get instant entry via a cafe in Nigeria onto the dark webs hit list of vulnerable souls who are then fleeced of their hard earned.

I met her on a train journey home after staying with my daughter. During a period in which the train was delayed it was raining and cold and I decided to sit in the stations waiting room. In which a larger-than-life lady began talking to me. She was very exuberant and somewhat eccentric and told me that she was psychic, and reading peoples tarot cards was her new age skill. She proudly told me that she had many famous clients, and had also appeared on foreign television shows.

Tarot cards have always scared the bejesus out of me, and I felt immediately uncomfortable. The very thought of the death and hangman cards being produced, and then being told that they have a positive meaning... I think not! As a child I was always fearful of anything remotely linked to divination, particularly tarot card readers and fortune tellers. So much so that when I visited the seaside and passed any dodgy little booths or tents that advertised either, I would take the widest berth possible. A good twenty feet was preferable, and whilst passing them I would ensure my gaze remained firmly fixed on anything that I considered to be safe.

Celeste was sitting opposite and began to join in with the conversation, as did a young lady who was going home to see her parents on a break from university. We all boarded the train and sat near one and other so that we could continue our conversation. The student disengaged after five minutes and put her headphones on, and I wished that I could do the same. As our journey came to an end, we exchanged phone numbers with a view to possibly meeting up for a coffee in the future. I thought little more of it and was just relieved to be home, and I didn't expect to see either of them again. However, a week or so later Celeste had contacted The

Empress who rang me, and we arranged to meet up for a cuppa and a chat.

The meeting was not entirely unpleasant but a little strange and I was very much the three's a crowd element. Both The Empress and Celeste rabbited for England and neither listened when the other spoke. And so, I took the role of marriage guidance counsellor, and when one ignored the other, I would repeat what the ignored party had just said to try and make the conversation more balanced. It worked a few times but after thirty minutes I gave up and just listened. The Empress was the more dominant of the two and was very arrogant and showed clear impatience, boredom and annoyance when she was not centre stage. It was clear from the get-go that she had a very strong sense of entitlement and you had to pay court to her. After a few hours we went our separate ways and I hoped that it was a one off. Sadly, not to be and The Empress began bombarding me with emails, phone calls and text messages. To such an extent that it was beginning to border on being a little creepy.

My final communication with her was after she had sent me an email in which she told me that she believed in curses and such like, and she had attached a photo of a delightful little book called " Curses and Maledictions". Curses were bad enough and I had no clue what a malediction was, so a google search enlightened me, it is a magical word or phrase uttered with the intention of bringing about evil. Enough said that was me permanently out of there, bricking it that some kind of occult retribution was coming my way. The phone and email block buttons were immediately pressed as was the addition of Psalm 91 to my daily prayers.

Which left me in touch with Celeste who instigated 90% of all communication with lengthy and very effusive emails with attachments recommending all manner of beautiful items many of which related to interior design. As well as mentioning all of the kind and caring acts she had done for others and absolutely anything that related to angels and angel numbers.

I had known her for about six weeks and was a little surprised by a response to a text that I had replied to. As you know I am particularly careful when replying to messages as they can easily be misconstrued. After the ten- minute rule I had very warmly and politely responded to her, and completely out of the blue, her response was like a rapid-fire machine gun. Listing a barrage of bullet points all relating to personal facts, none of which related to the previous text's contents. Her sign off was that she was very tired (drooping eyelids her words) and the first of many charming expressionless emojis. I truthfully had never received a text like it and however hard I tried to make sense of its contents and why she had fired it off I couldn't.

I saw her infrequently and she always instigated our meetings, which were usually at her house. She made constant apologies for the state of her home, which she clearly knew was a designers' Homes and Gardens paradise. And her professed adulation of her two cats didn't marry up with her constantly telling them to stop what they were doing (apart from breathing). Having a cup of tea and a cake was like watching an autopsy, the colour of the tea and laying out of the cake, was undertaken in a far too serious manner. If she had made a coroner's report in her diary when I left, I would not have been in the least bit surprised. If I spoke about myself for longer than two minutes, she would usually interrupt and would walk into the kitchen whilst I was mid- sentence. Her husband spent many hours in his garage and used to pop in and ask "Is it alright if I come in now?" And would joke that he was only permitted in on Celestes say so. I thought it was marital banter, but there was an underlying truth hidden by a smile and a very dry wit.

Once we sat in the garden, and he joined us for ten minutes, I expect it had been scheduled in, and he asked if I had a cat would I allow it in my bedroom. To which I replied yes as I was not fussy about things like that, and it was their home too. Celeste at this point was walking towards the house to get something from the kitchen, she turned round and glared at me and told me "If you expect us to remain friends, you seriously won't be going down that route".

On another occasion she showed me a group of framed photos which had been arranged on her beautiful sideboard. One was of her daughter whom I had met. She was completely unlike her mother and was very down to earth, streetwise easy to talk to and very attractive, and I warmed to her instantly. Her daughter was looking up at the camera with the saddest and most world-weary expression, if I could have reached into the photo to give her a hug I would have. Celeste used to often say how bitterly disappointed she was that her daughter hadn't married or had children. And spoke in very critical terms regarding her daughter's weight and appearance and behaviour in general. I used to think just be grateful that you have a child, when other people can't have children or have suffered a terrible loss.

There were another couple of niggles that didn't marry up with her self professed celestial status. One being she sent me an email about a note her husband had left on the door for any deliveries. He was dyslexic, and she relayed verbatim what he had written, and was clearly extremely annoyed about it. Everything had to be perfect and precise with regards to how she came across to others. I was a little unsure how to respond and replied that dyslexia had no bearing on personal intelligence and my ex-husband, and an uncle also had the condition.

It was clear that we had very little in common and gradually the situation came to a natural end. The Coronavirus R number had crept up pre second wave and although households could still mix, I thought it best not to. She had invited me round and I politely declined the offer and explained that when things were a little better it would be lovely to have a cuppa. A few minutes later I received one of her machine gun rude responses with drooping eyelids and expressionless emoji. Once again, she was rude and dismissive, and I wondered why she had remained in contact with me, it was time for me to take a step back from the situation.

Not long after we had first met I had told her about my unusual personality type, and I decided to respond by email and mention it once again. I sent the briefest attachment about The Advocate INFJ and hoped that she may pick up on some of the buttons that she was constantly pushing and perhaps it would give her a gentle nudge to be a little more considerate. I suggested that maybe she would like to do the Myers Briggs test as it was interesting and incredibly accurate. And I made a prediction with regards to a Myers Briggs Type she may be.

Her response was that she was too busy to look at the link as she was engaged in "far more interesting and proactive activities". She was extremely tired (drooping eyelids) and once more out came her favourite expressionless emoji.

I then had the light bulb moment and realized that there was little to no real substance behind her self professed selfless nature and it was simply words that she used to purvey a persona which was far from authentic. So, I decided to subtly highlight in a very carefully worded response that I fully understood just how busy she was with work and all of the good deeds that she did for others. And suggested that perhaps like me she was over tired and needed some time out. I apologized for sending the Myers Briggs link and told her that I understood it could be incredibly annoying when you receive them. This was to not so subtly highlight that she had sent me enough links to make five miles of chain fence. And finally, I brought up the dreaded emoji, and let her know that I had noticed its regular appearance and its meaning. And that I had presumed she didn't know what it meant as she was normally so precise.

I had a gut feeling it was going to expose her, but hoped to be proven wrong. Her response was very brief, stating she had done the Myers Briggs test, and was one of three possibilities. The one that I had put forward in my nice email (if she truly was all rainbows and roses an INFP The Mediator) then in her words " I could be the one with E in front the Champion and possibly the Entertainer, I could have checked more thoroughly but wasn't THAT (shouty emphasis) bothered". She clearly had taken a cursory look at the site and had picked a couple that reflected what she wanted to purvey. The highlighted emoji issue response was "Oh (expressionless emoji picture) to me means smug, contented or pleased!!!!!!So sorry if I misinterpreted". The overuse of exclamation marks said it all, she was not a happy bunny.

The following morning after my discovery I was quite literally told that I had to write a book, something that I had not once ever thought about, or ever considered doing.

If like me you like to know where you are heading, I aim to have the first 50% of the book dedicated to events and experiences which are related to narcissism, abuse and injustice.

And as for the following 50%?

I have learnt that surprises are not always a bad thing...

Song: The Safety Dance Men Without Hats

ROOM 2

The Tale of Two Elephants

The proverbial elephant in the room will incite a lot of collective false memories when people are too afraid or confused to question a narrative that is being presented to them. How my family of origin were perceived by the outside world was incredibly important to a few of its members. But from the earliest of ages, I was acutely aware of the disconnect between reality and what was purveyed to the outside world. My familial rose-coloured spectacles had not been issued and I had been mistakenly given a pair of x ray glasses. Ones that were able to see through a couple of Nelly's and their misguided mahouts.

My mother came from a middle-class background her father was a tall, dignified man, who reminded me of the actor David Niven. Throughout WW2 he was in the RAF and flew a Lancaster bomber and conducted many missions for Coastal and Bomber Command. Her mother was petite and beautiful and in her twenties was frequently told that she looked like the actress Merle Oberon. During the war she worked as a secretary for the MOD and had met her husband at an RAF party in Cornwall. They married and after the war brought a farm and had two daughters, mum being the eldest.

As a child mums behaviour affected the family dynamic in many different ways. She was awkward with regards to getting up in the mornings to such an extent that it caused chaos, resulting in her younger sister being regularly late for school. There was a general disregard for others, and she didn't fit into the family unit. Once she grabbed hold of her sister's head and repeatedly smashed it against the wall of the property. She had no intention of stopping and her mother had to pull her off. As a teenager whilst her mother was preparing the Sunday roast, she had become enraged about something and grabbed the carving knife from the kitchen table and brandished it at her terrified mother. Her parents both knew that there was something wrong and as a Christian my grandfather felt something was amiss on a spiritual level. The situation became so bad at one point he thought of discussing the matter with a priest. Which sounds like he was a religious zealot, but this could not have been further from the truth, he was a very calm, practical and logical man. Nothing could be done to remedy the bad behaviour and she remained attention seeking, rebellious and volatile, and as soon as she was able to leave home, she did so and moved to London. Throughout I will refer to her as mum or Brigitte as she aspired to be a model and although brunette, she had similar features to Brigitte Bardot.

One Christmas she came home to see her parents and sister with a new boyfriend, and on arrival her parents immediately noticed her normally thin waist had expanded. And they asked her if she was pregnant, and she admitted that she was. What was discussed over that Christmas I do not know, but her boyfriend left for home the following day and was never seen again. Shortly after the holidays mum discovered that he had married a lady who had recently given birth to his child a boy, and she was understandably heartbroken. Grandad was extremely angry by the way she had been treated and sent my father a very strongly worded letter, but of course nothing could be done to remedy the situation. I know that it was an upsetting time for all parties involved, but it was portrayed like a Greek tragedy. Extremely dramatic, and full to the brim with pathos, it was surprising that a film hadn't been made off the back of it. It was a sad situation but one that needed to be addressed with a far more pragmatic approach

When I arrived on the scene it was not long before I became aware of my surroundings and a few early memories have always remained with me, unchanged and are precisely as they happened. Events which are not particularly exciting and normally I would not relay them to anyone. They are only of importance with regards to the use of gaslighting by a couple of family members who have altered and denied reality, truth and facts to suit.

My earliest memory was at the tender age of no more than six- or seven-months. I was in a very large austere room with wood panelling on the walls and was sitting in a metal cot on pristine white sheets. The sun was shining through a large, sashed window which was open, and the net curtain was bellowing in the breeze and beyond the window I could see green foliage. It was extremely quiet and although I was alone, I wasn't in the least bit distressed. I had a little rubber doll lying beside me, who had thick light brown hair and was wearing a royal blue short sleeved mini dress, with white piping round the bottom and pearly white buttons down the front. I kept squeezing her arm and couldn't fathom how it could spring back to its original shape when I released my grip. I was to later discover that the sunny room was located in a children's home. A place that was not mentioned in detail with regards to specific timescales. But I know that whilst I was in the home mum had begun training to become a nurse.

Each weekend I stayed with my grandparents, with the view that eventually I would live permanently with my mother, when she was able to look after me. For one weekend visit I remember sitting in a large black and cream Silver Cross pram. And in front of me was a stuffed toy, a white dappled horse with black spots, wool mane and tail. It was a beautiful sunny day and my very first memory of gran. Who walked up to me and smiled, and after talking to me for a while she began to walk away. I wanted her to stay and picked up the horse and threw it out of the pram and much to my delight she returned.

Around the same time, I was with grandad in an old red brick outbuilding, watching him tie up newspapers with string on a wooden bench, which had lots of glass jars on with bits and bobs in. A fly had entered the building, and it began to irritate him. He grabbed a plastic fly swot which was the prettiest shade of jade green and eventually managed to kill it. I was intrigued by how fast he was moving and how happy he was when he had successfully hit his target.

Not long after this I was taken out of the Children's home and went to live with my mother and her new boyfriend in a rented bungalow. My first recollection of this property is waking up in a very dimly lit room and feeling anxious and alone. I knew that I was very wet, cold and uncomfortable and I felt incredibly thirsty. I stood up and looked around but instinctively knew that there was no point in crying, so I plonked myself back down. I needed to drink something and looked once more around the room. To my left was a table with a small brown glass bottle on, I reached through the bars of my cot and grabbed hold of it. Luckily the lid had not been placed back on, I took a swig and enjoyed the sugary fruity taste, so I finished the bottle. My thirst had been quenched and I went very soundly back into a very deep sleep. In hindsight I wonder whether it could have been a child sedative, probably not but I will never know. The NSPCC advert that had a little boy standing in a cot looking very sad with the commentary "Miles is a quiet baby" always resonates with me with regards to this memory.

In all honesty at this time, I don't remember any positive interactions just incidents that stood out. One being whilst watching Hectors House mums partner came into the living room with some fish and chips. I was passed some in a white wrapper and to my horror there was something moving in my fish. I screamed in disgust which they both found incredibly funny. Subsequently I still have an aversion to anything that remotely resembles a maggot.

During this time, I had my first experience of seeing the sea, I recall looking down at my feet and admiring a pair of pink jelly shoes that I thought were extremely pretty. I looked up from them and across to a vast expanse of something that I didn't recognize, the sea. Which was far too big for my liking, I was terrified and began to cry. The next thing I remember is flying and landing on a synthetic blanket in a pretty shade of blue with satin edging around it. Mums' boyfriend had been the source of my unrequested solo maiden flight. I clearly recall mum saying, "You shouldn't have done that she is too little". At least she had recognized that throwing me across the room was not remotely acceptable.

I spent an awful lot of time in the garden walking round in circles with a tin drum, I was alone but not at all distressed by the fact. Whilst in the garden one sunny day I felt that I needed water on my hair. I probably was dirty but it's doubtful that I would have known and perhaps I was just too hot. In the garden was a grey metal water tank on a low wooden platform that had water in. Somehow, I clambered up onto it and gave myself a quick head dunk. What I was doing unsupervised when I was so little is beyond me my safety was clearly of little to no importance.

At the end of the garden was a chain fence, which I often used to wander up to, and look at all that was happening beyond my confines. One day a couple and their two children a boy and girl began talking to me and they seemed very kind. I remember being pulled up over the fence and going to the beach with them and having a lovely big ice cream. When I mentioned the incident to her as an adult, she told me that I had been missing for an entire afternoon. I thought she may have said that she was concerned that I had been abducted, but all she purveyed was that she found the incident somewhat amusing.

We would often pass a small recreation ground which had a slide, some swings and a roundabout in it, I used to look longingly at the children playing and couldn't understand why I could not join them. But one day they stopped and asked me whether I would like to go on the roundabout. To which I shook my head, as I had always wanted to go on the little slide. They told me that I couldn't, and the roundabout would be far more fun. So reluctantly I stepped onto it and held on tightly to one of the curved bars that radiated out from the centre. The next thing I knew I was being spun round at breakneck speed and I was screaming at them to stop turning it. Frightened that I was going to fall off, I moved to the centre and sat down. Both were giggling whilst I shut my eyes tightly for what seemed like an absolute eternity. Eventually the amusement factor was lost and the roundabout came to a painfully slow halt. But their amusement was once more ignited as I stumbled off, barely able to stand up straight or walk in a straight line. Situations like this were the norm, but as luck would have it, I was soon to have some much-needed respite.

My grandparents had moved to a beautiful 18th century cottage in a different County, and we took a train to see them. On the journey I felt extremely hot, and I had great difficulty breathing either in or out. I was frightened and felt absolutely dreadful, whilst neither of them took any notice of my clear distress. Apparently, I had collapsed when I had arrived at my grandparents home. And was bed ridden for three weeks and had bronchial pneumonia. I awoke to see Gran smiling at me and she told me that a doctor was coming to see me, and his name was Doctor Foster. She proceeded to recite the rhyme Doctor Foster went to Gloucester in a shower of rain, he fell in a puddle right up to his middle and was never to be seen again.

Mum and her boyfriend had disappeared, and I was told much later that they had been absolutely disgusted at the state in which I was in. And they didn't think it was safe for me to be left in their permanent care. Unsurprisingly I did not miss either of them, and I felt peaceful, no longer ignored and very safe. And also a little shocked that I was allowed to speak and have fun with grown-ups. The good times commenced, and I have many beautiful memories of the months that I spent with them, too many to list but here are a couple. I had many idyllic walks in the local wood with my dear grandad, he would show me a wooden door in the riverbank and told me that it was a very special place, where fairies lived. I was allowed to go there and see it because I was such a good and special little girl. Although they never made an appearance, I never once doubted their existence, the wood was absolutely magical. Gran often used to do a little Scottish jig and sing Whoopsie Diddly Dandy Dee, which always made me chuckle. I would sit in the kitchen with her and watch her cook. I loved to make her giggle and could always set her off by pulling silly faces and singing made-up non sensical songs, usually mentioning the words poo and wee as you do! Once she started laughing it would set me off and we would both be beside ourselves chuckling away. She would tell me that I was a very naughty little girl for making herself lose control and that she was nearly wetting herself. This naturally enhanced my performance, and my goal was always to get her to that point.

When my grandfather used to leave the house for work in the morning, I would cling onto one of his legs as a bear would cling onto a tree trunk. He would continue to walk, get his coat and hat on by the door and I would only release my grip if he promised to see me before I went to bed. And so, they gave me the pet name Mishka which is Russian for little bear. Gran would often sing "Mishka is a very kind bear a great big nobly bear".

They owned a large blue record player and often used to play music in the home which I adored. The first single I distinctly remember being played was Wonderful World by Louis Armstrong. I found the words beautiful and much to my grandparent's amusement I used to sing along to it in my best and deepest Louis voice, which never failed to have them both in stitches.

My Sweet Lord by George Harrison was also regularly played, the lyrics resonated strongly with me, and they still do. I felt like it was my song and had been written especially for me. I completely understood the lyrics and I felt that I was in a place that was ok, but not my real and true home. Something far bigger and beautiful was out there for us all, and I wanted to live there and be with Jesus. It was a great comfort to know there was another "home" for us all, and someone was singing about it. I was only a little girl, so it wasn't a crush, but I used to look at Georges photo on my grandparent's Beatles album covers and think he was utterly beautiful in a very non worldly way. I was a little obsessed with George, the song and Jesus and I loved talking about them. So, gran asked me whether I wanted to learn a prayer that I would say every night before I went to sleep. And so, she taught me a prayer that was simple and short, which I said every night without fail.

Gentle Jesus meek and mild

Look upon a little child

God Bless.......

(A list of all my family members)

Thank You Lord

Amen

I have the sweetest little photo of me taken around the time of my George Harrison obsession. It was taken in the cottages living room by grans beloved nephew John who was a priest. I remember feeling incredibly peaceful around him, he was very calm, quietly spoken and kind. For my little photo shoot, I was wearing a mushy pea green coloured hand knitted jumper, and red tartan trousers. The photo purveys determination and a little soul wise beyond its years. I am looking directly at the camera, with my arms crossed and I refer to it as my "knowing photo". Life may have aged me, but it captures my core identity, and grounds me tremendously if I look at it. At the time it was taken I already had an awareness regarding this world and heaven. And understood that there were two dimensions, which were intertwined and there was also an area that lay between the two

One morning I was called into my grandparent's bedroom, and gran instructed me to sit beside her on the bed. I clambered up and sat next to her and she proceeded to tell me that I had to be a very brave little girl for her and grandad, and that I had to go and live with my mummy somewhere else. I replied, "No I don't want to you are my mummy". I kept repeating "You are my mummy" with the vainest of hopes that my insistence would change the situation. She held me close as I sobbed, and was in tears also, things were never going to be the same again for the knowing little soul.

Song: I'll Find My Way Home Jon Anderson & Vangelis

ROOM 3

Little Miss Sunshine to Cold Little Scott

From the safety and security of my grandparents' house I seemed to be instantaneously transported to a different location. One that could quite well have been on a different planet, as it was devoid of love, fun and compassion. I held my grans hand as we walked from their car into a Victorian terraced house, and into a large room with a patterned orange lino floor. The room was sparsely furnished and at the furthest end was an immaculately polished table with a bottle of apple squash placed in the centre. I was intrigued by the bottles lid, which was white and had deep grooves covering its circumference. It was out of proportion and covered at least three inches of the bottles neck, it looked like a hat, and I imagined placing it on a little dolls head.

A lady whom I vaguely recognized asked me whether I wanted a drink and I replied, "no thank you". I looked away from the table and around the room and my grandparents were no longer standing beside me. There were no goodbyes, and they seemed to have just vanished into thin air. In hindsight it was for the best, for witnessing them leave would have left me with an indelible and sad memory, one that would have stayed with me far longer than a moment of confusion. I became immobile and froze almost immediately. My lone Scott of the Antarctic expedition had begun, and I no longer had the adequate clothing to protect me.

I returned swiftly back to silent mode as I knew that it was inadvisable to speak. It was rare for me to utter more than the odd yes or no to my new parents. It was only if I was extremely distressed, and I couldn't process a problem alone that I would instigate a conversation.

One such occasion was when I was eleven and my teacher had decided to talk to the girls in the class about breast cancer, which in hindsight was incredibly bad timing. She explained that we must all be very aware of any lumps growing in our breasts. Very true and extremely important, but not when you are a pubescent girl. I was going to die, as there were very distinct hard lumps in my skinny little chest, I was absolutely petrified. I kept the fact that I was going to die for what seemed like an eternity, but it was probably no more than a week. My head began to feel like it was going to explode, and I knew that I was going to have to tell mum that I was extremely worried about my health.

I agonized over what words I could use that would allow me to swiftly and succinctly explain my health concerns. And, how to choose a good moment that wouldn't annoy her. I watched her in the kitchen from the living room, making a cup of Camp coffee in-between drawing on yet another cigarette, and I could not contain my fear a moment longer. I waited until she made momentary eye contact with me and blurted out "Mum I'm dying". She responded coldly "Why do you think such a stupid thing"? And on the longest out breath I could manage, I explained that my teacher had told us if we had lumps in our breasts, it could be cancer and I had a few big lumps. She simply replied, " I was being bloody ridiculous, and it was because I was changing into a woman". Enough said, her response was more than sufficient, I was going to live thank goodness.

With regards to puberty many girls of narcissistic mothers are denied any information about bodily changes. My take on it is as well as being a form of emotional neglect, it is a reminder that a younger female is closing in on them and has the potential to blossom and be authentic. My stepfathers mum helped me with all that I needed to know regarding puberty and was so terribly sweet, I cannot thank her enough for all that she did for me.

I remember our very first meeting at her local train station, I was greeted by the warmest smile, and she reached out her hand to me, which I was more than happy to take. We walked up what seemed at the time to be a never-ending hill and much to my relief we eventually reached a very neat modern terraced house. On entering the houses living room there was a man sitting at the dining room table with dark hair, a tanned complexion, and dark eyes. He was wearing a brown and orange checked lumberjack shirt and greeted me with the warmest of smiles. He was my new uncle and was not in the least bit like my stepfather in looks or his mannerisms. Gran told me that he was the spit of her late husband who had died at the end of WW2. He was quiet and very kind with an extremely dry sense of humour and worked as a self-employed builder.

Gran was a wonderful lady and I had so much love and respect for her, it must have been incredibly hard living in a small close-knit community and suddenly having a new grandchild thrust upon you. One who has no genetic connection, but she immediately embraced me as her own grandchild. I cannot think of anyone who looks like her, but I will give you a description because she thoroughly deserves one. She was petite and had small but perfect features, with very good skin, a beautiful smile and kind blue eyes. Her grey hair was always very neatly set, and she loved Yardley Freesia perfume. She was a brilliant cook and an absolute stickler for routine, which I loved as it made me feel safe and secure.

At this time mum worked very infrequently as a bank nurse, A regular position would not have suited her, and she was able to pick and choose her shifts to suit. Her medical training and knowledge were never applied at home. How she could go to work as a nurse, when her own children didn't receive rudimentary medical care made no sense at all to me. I often thought about it, along with a million other paradoxes, which should have not been given valuable head space. Oh, to have just thought about what outfit to put my Barbie in, and other much more important things such as the ultimate French plait to show off your mum's skills at school.

Once I had a very large stye on my top eyelid, it had made the lid completely swell and was not localised to one area. It was extremely sore and although styes do not normally require treatment, a trip to the doctors was necessary. Not to be though and nurse Brigitte decided to attend to the problem herself. She summoned me to the bathroom and had filled the sink full of hot water and had a dirty rough flannel in her hand. I knew that something had to be done about it, so I walked over to her with a great deal of trepidation. She roughly grabbed my chin with one hand and slapped the flannel with a great deal of force on to my swollen eye, to which I winced in pain. That really annoyed her, and she screamed "I am doing you a bloody favour you ungrateful little bitch you should be grateful, and this is how you repay my kindness" She then grabbed hold of my head and pushed my face into the sink, knocking my forehead against the hard enamel. I managed to wriggle free from her and jumped down the flight of stairs in three leaps and bolted outside.

I had regular earaches and often had pus oozing out from the infected ear, it is a miracle that there has been no permanent hearing damage, as I was never taken to the doctors for antibiotics. Our diet was absolutely appalling, and it was not due to financial poverty but simply because she couldn't be bothered to cook. A usual meal would be cheap fishfingers or reconstituted meat such as turkey burgers served with overcooked watery mashed potatoes and luke warm value baked beans. There was no nutritional value to the food, and I used to frequently have boils on my legs and abscesses in my nose. Grandad would regularly buy me a stash of blue boil plasters which were impregnated with magnesium sulphate paste to draw them out. The house was filthy, the bedding was dirty, and our clothes were washed infrequently. Brigitte always had cats, but they were never given flea treatment, and there was usually a heavy infestation of fleas throughout the house. You could actually see them jumping on the carpets, no microscope was needed to verify their presence. They took a particular liking to me, and my legs were covered in bites during summers flea season.

My brother and I wore dirty clothes that were far too small for us, many of which had scorch marks on from the iron, I would rather have had creased clothes but the fact that the iron was used showed a degree of effort. There was never any change of season attire and in winter my legs were always cold as I only possessed a couple of skirts, woolly tights or trousers were not an option. However, Brigitte always wore decent clothes; and would regularly return from the largest department store in town ladened down with carrier bags. Ross and I used to watch her unpack them, hoping that there would be something in them for us, but there never was.

My best friend Julia's mother Lynne once suggested to Brigitte that I join the Girls Brigade along with her daughter. Mum was extremely annoyed that she had been put on the spot and had to agree for appearances sake. I knew that somehow; I would look different and there would be an element of payback, and I was right. Firstly, she went and brought some navy material and hand stitched a skirt made freestyle without a pattern and sewn with white cotton in very large sparse stitches. A contender to win garment of the week on Great British Sewing Bee, I suspect not. Particularly with a hem that was two inches higher at the front than the back, Esme would have had an absolute fit! Luckily the blazer and cap couldn't be sabotaged but she had a field day with the skirt. I went once and the following week she decided to include an iron shaped scorch mark for added effect, that was the clincher, and I didn't attend again.

Directly opposite our house I had a friend called Joe who was a couple of years older than me. His parents were lovely, one was a teacher and the other a lecturer at the local college. On one visit his mum told me that she had a surprise for me. She had made the most beautiful dress in white cotton with a poppy print in shades of red and royal blue. It had smocking stitch in the same colour thread as the poppies on the bodice, a pie frill collar and long sleeves with frills around the cuffs. It must have taken many hours to make. I remember skipping round the entire playground when I proudly wore it the following day for school. I was as pleased as punch to wear such a beautiful dress that was pristine white and smelt as fresh as a daisy. I had my Princess for the day moment and savoured every second of my victory skip.

If someone shows me a kindness to this day, I still feel a little overwhelmed, whatever its size it always touches my heart. I know I often over thank people and a little of that is related to my mum she had the usual narcissists "sense of entitlement". She would receive gifts from people and never say thank you. She would respond with "that's nice", or "I like it ". As an adult I thought it quite funny waiting for an impossible word that most of us use regularly, I think she may have self-destructed if it had accidently slipped out.

Anything to do with a child's hygiene was never actioned or monitored by her, whether it was washing your body, cleaning your teeth or washing and brushing your hair. When I realised at the age of around seven that I was supposed to have a bath at least once a week, I used to ask whether I could have one. It was 50/50 as to whether I could or not, but when I was able to, it was usually after she had taken one, and I had to use the same water which I was not keen on.

Gran loved washing and brushing my hair, and I thoroughly looked forward to my pampering sessions. She would place a pale pink fluffy towel which had been warmed on the radiator onto the bathroom cabinet. Johnson's Baby shampoo and a wide toothed comb were also laid neatly onto the soft towel. I barely felt her little hands as she gently washed my long hair. It was like having a gentle Indian head massage and used to make me feel very sleepy and incredibly calm. My squeaky clean long brown hair was then blow dried with the strangest looking hairdryer that I am sure used to be plugged into the light bulb bayonet of a ceiling light, I can remember it hanging down and I had to sit directly underneath, goodness that sounds archaic. The final part of her salon treat was a brush with her mother's silver hairbrush, which had to be done for exactly 100 strokes.

I can only remember mum brushing my hair once, when I was between the age of six or seven. She was sitting on the sofa and asked me to sit between her legs on the floor. I was hesitant but sat down and was extremely surprised when she began to brush my hair. She began brushing very gently and did this for quite some time and I began to feel unusually relaxed. Suddenly the tempo changed, and she began brushing with a great deal of force and pressure. The brushes bristles were metal with rubber nodules on their tips, many of which were missing. I pulled my head away and got a whack with the brush for good measure.

The reason for my grooming session was soon to be revealed, she told me that a man was coming to take a photo of me and Ross. I asked what for, and she told me that it was for a Miss Pears competition, and she might win some money, and that I had to smile at him, when he asked me to. I was given a very pretty needle cord pinafore dress with a paisley print and a very clean white frilly blouse, a pair of black patent shoes and finally I was issued a pair of much dreamed of black woolly tights. I remember being so happy wearing clean clothes, but after the photo shoot I did not see my pretty outfit again. The photo is in my album, and I have the weakest little smile on my face, whilst biting my bottom lip, holding onto my brother who is on the point of tears. Not the best photo and Brigitte didn't get her winnings, what a shame but I knew I wouldn't have got a cut, and she would have gone straight to the local department store and cleared the makeup department of all its stock, particularly the lipstick.

However, she did get her revenge very shortly after. I had long brown hair and one day after school she said that she wanted to do something that would make me look much prettier. I was intrigued as to what but was quite frankly up for anything that may make me more popular at school. I sat down as she requested and was given the most hideous medieval monk style haircut; it truthfully could have been no worse and was very clearly deliberate.

Suffice to say that being almost mute, wearing odd clothes, having a hair style like Ann Widdecombe, stinking to high heaven and having large sad eyes it was a God given that I was going to be a target of bullying by the schools "mean girls". The main and unrelenting taunt was "what big eyes you have" from Red Riding Hood. It took me years to realise the best retort was "what a big mouth you have, so shut it".

Brigitte used to have a perverse delight in making me gag and my nemesis food was pork belly. Which was cooked in a casserole dish for about forty minutes with just water and a stock cube for flavour. The fatty part looked and tasted like lard, and I only had to look at it and would dry gag. She knew I hated it and subsequently it was made at least once a week to upset me. Gran was aware of this and once when they dropped me off after staying with them, my favourite meal had been prepared as a welcome home treat.

They gave me a kiss goodbye and I was filled with dread at the prospect of eating the meal. I said, "Please mum I can't eat it" but she insisted that I had to and was being verbally abusive. Suddenly the door opened, and in walked gran who said, " I am so sorry to interrupt but I think I have left my glove behind; Brigitte please don't make her eat that you know just how much she hates it". Many years later she told me that they had sat in the car at the end of the road for five minutes and came back because they knew that mum would try and force me to eat it.

My younger brother and I rarely brought what limited friends we had back to the house, and never for tea. It's not the greatest look when fleas are jumping out of your mash potato. I didn't think fleas had a penchant for King Edwards, but there was so many of the little blighters they had to land somewhere. The potatoes were so waterlogged by rights they should have drowned.

Brigitte rarely got out of bed before 11 am, her sleeping habits had not improved since her childhood. When my younger brother started school, I used to get him up, dress him and make his breakfast. We had a coal fire and in winter porridge was a good filling breakfast. If there were no available matches to light the gas cooker, I would get a long piece of newspaper and form it into a taper. Go to the open fire with its dying embers, light the paper, leg it to the kitchen and then press and turn the hobs knob to light the ring. It was extremely difficult getting the timing right, it was a fine balance between losing the flame or burning myself, but I always succeeded.

My brother was not on the receiving end of emotional or physical abuse; however, he was neglected with regards to general hygiene, medical care and he witnessed inappropriate events. Although he was treated far better than me it was still bad for him, and I think as an adult it has affected him far more than it did me. He often utilized his elevated position for his own benefit, but I understood that the role had been assigned to him and not one that he had asked for. I used to mentally refer to him as "The Golden Boy" which was pretty apt as "Golden Child" is the term used for a narcissist mothers' favourite child. Although as a child he was always allowed to do precisely what he wanted with no reprimand, I loved him very much regardless of how differently we were treated.

Brigitte always spoke in a monotone voice, very slowly and loudly as if she was talking to a person who did not speak her native tongue. She clearly presumed that all people were stupid, and she needed to enlighten them with her superior knowledge. However, if any of her captive audience didn't play ball, she would speak very rapidly as if she was struggling to breathe and on the point of complete collapse. When I was older, I could do a very good impression of her, which always made my brother giggle.

I was her personal listener and frequently heard very inappropriate conversations about men and her sex appeal. Half of the time I had no clue what she was talking about, but used to nod, listen and agree. Sometimes it would go on for over an hour. I used to think if I listen to her for as long as possible, I will eventually get in her good books, and she would leave me alone for a while. Of course, that never happened, I was on a hiding to nothing, but I never stopped trying or hoping.

She regularly preened herself in front of the mirror, with me standing by her side, it was exactly like the scene from the film "Mommie Dearest". She used to ask me "Don't I look beautiful"? As I had no option but to bolster her ego, my set response was "You look very pretty". But when I was fourteen, I decided to tell her the truth. She was getting ready for one of her regular air base pulling missions, and was wearing a tight leopard print dress, which clearly was her nod to Bet Lynch. The same question and I dropped the long overdue truth bomb "No you look really cheap", and boy did it feel good. She went immediately into one of her histrionic hyperventilating melt downs, but I was well used to them and for the very first time I totally ignored her behaviour.

She would lash out at me in particular when things were not going to plan. I would get kicked on the top of my legs, and have my hair pulled. Her favourite punishment was to grab hold of my hands and dig her nails into the inside most delicate part of my wrists, this left deep nail marks that took a while to disappear. Once whilst I was queuing to enter a lesson in middle school my teacher pulled me to one side because she had noticed them. And she asked me "What are the marks on your wrist"? I felt dirty and embarrassed that she had noticed them, so I simply replied, "The cat scratched me". However, being physically assaulted was the lesser of the two evils, for me it was far less damaging than the continual emotional abuse.

I began to feel what I mentally referred to as my "Not at home feeling", which was terrible. I struggled between trying to remain present and then the strangest feeling of not being in my own body. I know now that this was a state of disassociation and not a childhood out of body experience. I used to stare in the mirror trying somehow to reconnect with my reflection. I felt fragmented and I noticed my sad eyes, with dark circles underneath them and a mysterious black tide mark around my neck, I knew logically it was me, but somehow felt it wasn't. I was terribly frightened and hated feeling so distant. Once I felt so numb that I repeatedly banged my right hand against a wall, and I swear that I didn't feel a single thing.

I felt extremely unwell, but I never stopped saying my little prayer before I went to sleep. And although two people on my family prayer list had hurt me, my mum and stepdad always had a God Bless. I never once doubted that somehow one day it would all stop because God was in my corner. His "little child" may have been rendered a little too meek and mild, but she was never going to give in. There was still a spark of determination in me that never could be completely extinguished. I knew one day it would ignite and become a warm glow that would comfort me like nothing else ever truly could.

My grandparents picked me up whenever they could. And I stayed with them during most school holidays. They began asking me lots of questions with regards to what was happening at home. Which I was reluctant to answer as I presumed that because mum was their child, and she was an adult that I wouldn't be believed. I vaguely dropped a couple of hints as to what was happening, but not in a great deal of detail. I always began to feel better when I was with them, and I felt "at home" again both mentally and physically. One morning at breakfast they said that there was an important question they wanted to ask me. Which was would I like to live with them forever? My heart leapt I cannot tell you how happy I was, and I replied "yes, yes please when can I come?" They replied as soon as they could sort it, and hopefully it wouldn't be too long. I asked whether I would still be able to see my brother, to which they replied yes. I was told not to say anything as it was an important secret.

I went back to Antarctica with a warmth in my heart and a down jacket on already for my departure. And it must have shown, my expressionless face showed hope. I was in the living room, and I was dreaming of my escape, and it felt wonderful. Mum must have been watching me, and as narcissists can read every little facial nuance, she knew something was afoot. And she proceeded to ask me "what's the matter with you, why are you smiling"? I replied that I wasn't, and that I was just concentrating on something. She asked again, and I gave her precisely the same reply. She then told me that she didn't believe me and that I was lying, which of course I was. Rather stupidly I then blurted out, " I am going to go and live with gran and grandad". This was met with a prolonged stoney silence which I thought could be positive. But then to my dismay she replied, " You bloody well are not, where the hell have you got that stupid idea from"? I replied truthfully "You don't want me, and they do, I love them very much". Her reply was brutal and to the point, she looked me straight in the eyes and said, "No I don't want you, and I don't love you, but they are not having you, what would people think about me, I don't want you to ever be happy". I found out many years later, they had asked her, but she had point blank refused, and had told them if it happened, they would never see my brother again. My grandparents were extremely honourable, and they never would have deserted my brother.

If I see a child around now, that looks too thin, is unkempt and has dirty inappropriate clothing, or looks too sad and world weary for their young years. My heart yearns to pick them up and fix all their problems and worries just as all my grandparents did for me. If I ever am lucky enough to win the lottery, I will secretly do something very big for children who need help in anyway.

I consider myself extremely lucky in the scheme of things, because my case of abuse in comparison to some poor souls is minimal. The one which does distress me greatly is "The Polish Salt Boy Case" Daniel Pelka who suffered terribly. He was starved and fed salt and must have died in such terrible pain. He was far too special for this cruel world, and I am sure he is at peace with the angels, having the biggest cuddle with a belly full of all his favourite food.

God bless Daniel and all of the little children in heaven and around the world who for far too many reasons are suffering at the hands of sick strangers and family members. "Human Beings" who should never have had children or be allowed anywhere near them.

Song: Bring Me to Life Evanescence

ROOM 4

The Thespian

My stepfather had a slight build and was much shorter than Brigitte, in later life he reminded me of the actor Tony Robinson, only with regards to his appearance. He attended RADA when he left school, which was unusual as he came from a working-class background. He was very talented and was given a scholarship after an audition. His acting ability was not only contained to the stage, he was also able to quickly adapt and morph into whatever role was required of him when relating to people on a personal level. He could play many different parts, and all were extremely convincing. However, this skill did not need to be utilized at home, and he was almost unrecognizable behind closed doors. With only the living room curtains, no stage, audience or luvvie friends to heap adoration and praise on him there was no point. Without the stage lights and make-up, he was morose, quiet and regularly depressed, almost as if he was devoid of any emotion. He rarely showed anger, but when he did his temper was explosive and came without warning. He was usually found in the house sitting glued to the television, chain-smoking and with a face on him like a well smacked arse.

I saw him act several times in leading roles in amateur productions at the local theatre. He once played the part of the King in the musical The King and I. On the death bed scene, I cried because I believed that the lovely King had really died. For a couple of hours, he was someone that I actually liked. He was an exceptionally good actor, who never got his lucky break. This was a fact and regardless of his behaviour, one that I would never take away from him.

From the earliest of ages, I could see the man behind the mask and although it was clear to me, most people believed the alternative plot that was being presented to them. He was always charm personified particularly around my grandparents, genial, intelligent and a little sycophantic. When he and mum got divorced this continued, and there was no point in me ever telling them otherwise.

His real personality coming to the fore was the reason I found out about my absent natural father at the tender age of five. For some reason only known to his self, I had done something terribly wrong and had deserved to be chastised. Maybe it was a rehearsal for his latest leading role as an ex-champion league footballer, and I was to play a contemporary role as the ball. In the rented house where we lived, two downstair rooms had been knocked into one, and at the dividing point there was a brick plinth which was used to pile up books. It became the goal post, and I was being dribbled gradually into the back of the net.

Eventually I managed to get away and ran up two flights of stairs to the spooky old attic. Needs must, I wanted to get as far away as possible from him and a supernatural encounter was preferable. I sat on the attic floor and sobbed my heart out I didn't understand what I had done, in fact I didn't understand anything anymore. After a while Brigitte came up the stairs and I asked her, "why doesn't my daddy love me?". Her response was simple and direct "Because he is not your dad" to which I asked, "Where is mine then?". Her reply was "He lives miles away and does not want to know you". I distinctly remember thinking "What a lucky man he was that he didn't have to see her". She turned on her heels and left me crying, whilst I tried to process what she had just told me.

Although they were partners in crime with regards to their shared dislike of me, as a couple they had very little in common and regularly fought. Mum used to instigate fights with him and once stubbed a cigarette out on his hand. He managed to push her off and she fell over in a dramatic heap on the floor. The following day she went to the doctors and told them that she was a victim of domestic abuse. Throughout her life she has pulled the victim card, and many years later when she moved abroad, she did precisely the same again but on a far grander scale.

There was only very minimal interaction between me and my stepdad just silence. Apart from Christmas when he made an effort, not always with my presents though. I wasn't his and he let me know in countless ways. One year when I was around seven years old, I had put in my annual request to Father Christmas for a cuddly Snoopy. I couldn't wait for Christmas to arrive and have a cuddle with my new toy. The big day arrived, and we were summoned to their bedroom where the presents had been laid out. I was immediately handed my single present from Father Christmas. I eagerly unwrapped it and was horrified to find a bendy rubber Snoopy. Ever the optimist I decided that Santa wouldn't have made such a terrible mistake, and it must have been a magic one. And if I wished hard enough it would miraculously grow some very much-needed fur. Ross had a sit on red toy tractor and racing car, it was like his own personal Hamleys in their bedroom. Presents were piled up on the floor and the bed, most of which were for him from an overly generous Father Christmas.

I am writing this fairly, so I am not going to relay solely negative experiences. One Christmas Eve we were sitting at the dining table, and he secretly rang a bell, and convinced my brother and I that Santa and his reindeer were directly overhead, which was magical. Also, on Christmas Day Brigittes sleep patterns remained unaltered and she laid in bed for as long as possible. We were not allowed to open our presents until she deemed us with her presence. My stepdad did get up at the same time as us which I really appreciated. It would have been really strange if we had been left to our own devices on a morning that is about love, family and togetherness.

And now onto a very odd experience...

Mum was out when I arrived home from school one afternoon, and he was preparing tea. Butterscotch Angel Delight was my favourite treat, and I could eat bucket loads of the stuff. On entering the living room, it was a little disconcerting as he made a point of drawing my attention to him. He must have been reading the script for David Copperfield and was reading the part of Uriah Heep and said with a very slimy and somewhat creepy grin " Look what I have made especially for you" and he pointed towards the dining table. I looked across and down at a glass bowl which seemed to be filled with my favourite dessert. I was immediately suspicious and wondered why he had done something so nice, and I asked him what it was. He replied, " Just try it", and so, I placed a loaded dessert spoon into my mouth. It was mustard, which I immediately spat out and ran upstairs to rinse my mouth out.

And now to the bit that "could have been worse" which is true but a justification to minimise any form of abuse.

I was ten years old and at middle school and remembered during a morning class that I had PE in the afternoon and hadn't brought my black plimsolls with me. I rushed back home in my dinner break to collect them. On arrival my stepfather was sitting on his TV chair, which was a very typical 1970's design. The main body was tan PVC, with a brown, orange and cream striped boucle fabric seat cushion. It was a sunny day, and I can remember looking at the dust motes caught in the sun rays.

He saw me enter the room and I didn't expect him to speak as it was not the norm for him to do so. But he spoke and requested that I went over to him, caught off guard and confused I asked him "Why?". And then he gave me what felt like an order "Take your knickers off". I asked him again "Why?" and he replied, "Just do as you are told".

I thought that I must have done something terrible, because it wasn't what he usually did as a punishment. Although I knew that I hadn't done anything wrong I felt that I had no choice but to obey him because he sounded deadly serious. I quickly removed my knickers and walked over to him. He told me to lay across his legs and he pulled the back of my skirt up. In readiness I clenched my backside ready for a good old smack as it was all that I expected. The anticipated smack didn't happen and the next thing I felt was him stroking my backside for what seemed like an eternity. I didn't say a word because I didn't dare, I just froze. When his hand stopped moving, I jumped off him and felt stunned.

I put my PE knickers back on, grabbed my plimsolls and ran out of the house and back to school. I didn't understand it, but I knew that it wasn't right, and was in shock. I switched off for a while and tried to compartmentalize the event and was extremely careful around him. I became hypervigilant scanning each room before I entered, and only if someone was in the room with him would I enter, and then I'd stick like shit to a blanket round them.

They divorced when I was twelve years old and just prior to them splitting up they had a chat with Ross and I about the situation. We knew that it was on the horizon because all they did was argue, and we wanted it to happen asap. Whilst engrossed in a Saturday afternoon showing of Chitty Chitty Bang Bang we were asked to turn off the television because they both had something very important to ask us.

Mum proceeded to deliver the news and asked us who we wanted to live with when they divorced. My stepdad was going to move back home with his mum and brother, and she would stay in the rented house. I immediately replied, "Gran and Grandad" and Ross answered simply "Dad" which spoke volumes. I was told that my choice was not an option and that I had to choose one of them. I conducted the fastest mental risk assessment ever, do I continue to live with her and all that it entailed, or put myself at risk with my stepfather? It was an impossible choice, and then the fact that my gran and uncle would be in the same house swung it for me I chose him, as it was the lesser of two evils. Nothing ever came of the discussion though and Ross and I stayed with her and nothing more was said about where we would live. In hindsight it probably was because there would not have been enough room in grans house. Nor would it have been fair on her looking after her two sons and two young children.

He moved out and I immediately felt better, as being on tenterhooks and checking your surroundings constantly to see whether you were safe was incredibly exhausting. He lived in the next County with his mum and brother, and we went there once a fortnight to see him. Ross was always with his dad whilst I gave him the widest berth possible. My gran must have thought I was a limpet, as I was her little shadow and almost glued to her side. I had made a personal vow that I would never tell her what had happened, I wanted to protect her and my little brother. I never thought anything untoward could ever happen again as I was so careful but unfortunately to a lesser degree it did.

One Sunday early evening, he had dropped us off home and we were saying goodbye in the living room. Mum was standing next to me, and Ross and my stepfather were standing opposite us. My stepfather went to kiss me goodbye, which I absolutely hated. I used to turn my cheek as far away as possible, if I had been able to rotate my head a full 90 degrees I would have. Completely out of the blue whilst I was turning my face away from him, something slimy and disgusting had been pushed into my mouth, I realized it was his tongue and I felt sick. I jumped back and immediately ran upstairs and grabbed a red flannel that probably had more bacteria on than a petri dish which had been cultivating for at least a year. I didn't care though and I put water on it and scrubbed my lips till all the surrounding area was bright red and then rinsed my mouth with handfuls of cold water. I heard the front door close and knew that Brigitte must have seen what had just happened. I ran downstairs and said to her "Dad just stuck his tongue in my mouth, you must have seen you were standing close to me, I feel really sick" her response was simply "So".

I could not understand why these incidents had happened and the only conclusion I could come to was that because I had large and doleful eyes, this had led my stepfather to do what he had done. I thought that somehow, I must have given him an impression that was wrong and therefore it was my fault. I used to wonder whether there was an operation that I could have that would reduce the size of my eyes, which is sad. And looking back at my childhood photos my eyes were not disproportionate to my face and to be honest, they were beautiful.

As I got further into my teenage years it reached the point when my fortnightly visits tailed off. I still visited my gran and uncle, and I avoided him as much as I could. I was no longer a child, and he knew that if he came near me again, he would be the recipient of a swift backhander. I felt creeped out by him, and he always used to call me "love" like butter wouldn't melt in his mouth. He did nothing further to me, and if anything, he was sickly sweet around me. This I felt was very calculated to try and invalidate what really happened and to disguise his true personality. During visits I used to watch him "perform" with all the locals, he was the genial pub quiz master, charity event organizer and all-round good egg.

I truly felt nothing towards him and strangely I felt pity for him because he had invented a persona which was not authentic. I wondered just how tiring it must be to have to keep the facade up. When Michael Jackson was being investigated, he brought the subject up over dinner and he passionately defended him. It was all a little odd as we hadn't brought the subject up, and it felt almost as if he was defending himself.

He often told me he was working with someone who was absolutely gorgeous, and that he fancied them, but they were far too young. Once I asked him just precisely how young, and he replied seventeen, he was in his late fifties. As a child I once was looking for something that I had mislaid and looked under their marital bed. I was shocked to find a pornographic magazine with photos of very young girls aged about twelve partly clothed in school uniforms. I doubted that he would have behaved inappropriately with anyone but me. But I suspected that he may have looked at indecent images of under aged girls online. He was forever changing and upgrading his computer and I wondered why. He once sold me one on the cheap and it worried me that it may have had something unpleasant on it's hard drive.

Once my dear gran had died, I really did cut back contact, but could not completely because of my younger brother and also because of Faye. This was always a great source of worry for me, and I was always on high alert with regards to her safety. When she had just turned three, I explained to her that no one must ever touch her in certain special areas. And if someone ever did and told her not to tell that she must tell me and nothing bad would ever happen to either of us. She was a bright little girl, and she did understand what I had told her. A conversation that was repeated every now and again as subtly as I was able to, until I knew it had been fully logged and understood. He asked on several occasions whether she could stay with him alone between the ages of five and eleven and I always made an excuse for her not to. She was only allowed to be alone with him on shopping trips or anywhere that was a public setting until the age of 14 when she did go camping with him, which was not ideal in hindsight. It was a terrible situation and I managed it as best as I was able, sadly life has no manual with regards to situations like this.

He and my younger brother had a relationship that was very unsettled it swung regularly between bouts of them being as thick as thieves, to both of them saying that they couldn't stand each other. After one major bust up my brother said to me "Kim you will never understand, just how manipulative dad is". I did but I could not say my hands were tied, I had no voice.

Time moves on and it does truly heal, you do not forget, but other events supersede past hurts and if you can, you must try and move on. I had, and I was not afraid of him, he was an old man who latterly suffered from a heart condition. The last time I saw him I had moved to a different part of England and had rented a holiday cottage to see mum and Ross, my youngest brother was at university.

Brigitte decided that a game of pitch and putt would be a good idea as she lived close to a course and regularly practised. Ross said it would be nice if his dad came along too. We all met up and my stepfather looked extremely ill, I felt very sorry for him as he struggled to walk round the course. Brigitte was getting the needle as she was by far the worse player, this was exacerbated by me getting the ball straight on the green every hole, I have no clue how as I had only played it a couple of times previously.

My brother was having a rough time and was talking constantly about himself, completely oblivious to the fact his father looked at death's door. At the end of the game my brother and his father left for home. I was extremely polite and thanked him for coming and I genuinely wished him good health. I had no intention of ever divulging what had happened to anyone there was no need. Sometimes it's best for all to let sleeping dogs lie, but sadly that was not to be.

    Song: Hey Little Girl by Icehouse

ROOM 5

The Secret Kick

At the beginning of our tour, I mentioned gaslighting which is an insidious form of psychological abuse and was a regular tactic used by my mother. The most distressing example happened when I was approximately eight years old. I had returned home from school and my younger brother was in the kitchen with his hand in a paper bag from the local bakery. He had just finished eating a sausage roll, and around his mouth was a huge amount of flaky pastry. Mum had followed me into the room no more than a few seconds later. Looking at the bag on the worktop she screamed "who has been eating those rolls, they are mine"? I replied immediately "you saw me just come in; it wasn't me it was Ross". The situation quickly escalated as I tried to explain like some sort of child barrister that it was physically impossible to have eaten one in ten seconds and Ross had crumbs all over his face. She was furious that I was able to logically defend myself and was incandescent with rage. And stormed into the living room to get the Bible from the book platform. She had done it a couple of times previously and it is a terrible thing to do to a child.

When I saw a documentary about the singer Prince this had also happened to him, and I suspect it has happened to many more children. She held the bible close to her chest and kept repeating I was a bad and wicked child for lying to her, and God would always be on her side, I was evil, and the devil was inside me. When she first did it, I was absolutely terrified because I thought that by her using a book that I considered pure and sacred against me somehow, I would be cursed by her words. As she screamed at me, I imagined myself interrupting her and telling her that the sky was blue, and the grass was green, and I knew that she would still have called me a liar.

I didn't have a clue what to do and went upstairs to my secret stash of loose change that grandad had given me. Emergency money that was to be used if I ever wanted to talk to them secretly from the local call box. I grabbed about 30ps worth of coins, knowing that I had no option but to replace the sausage rolls. I cried whilst I was walking to the shop, and whilst I asked for them in the bakery. I paid for them and walked to the zebra crossing to cross the main road. I looked to my left and a car had stopped, and the driver beckoned me to cross. Not looking to the right, I put my foot into the road and a car clipped my foot and I fell over. I was not concerned about my throbbing foot and was far more worried about getting home and hobbled towards my destination as quickly as I was able. On arrival I placed the sausage rolls on the kitchen worktop and sat down. Within minutes there was a knock on the door and mum answered, and I heard a male voice saying, " I hope you don't mind but I have just followed your little girl home and she is extremely distressed, is she alright"? To which mum replied in her sweetest most convincing "mumsy" voice, that I was fine, and I was just a very "sensitive" child.

Sensitive in that context of course often means fully aware of all the lies and BS which is around them. I am admittedly sensitive and fulfil many of the criteria necessary to be considered a Highly Sensitive Person, however a couple do relate to being an INFJ also. Please excuse the self-indulgent I's which are a pet hate of mine.

- I avoid violent movies or TV programmes as they make me feel extremely unsettled.

- I am deeply moved by beauty in nature or the human spirit.

- I become overwhelmed in noisy or crowded environments.

- I have a physical need for down time especially after a hectic day.

- I think very deeply and have a rich and sometimes complex inner life.

- I have a strong startle reflex if I hear a sudden loud noise.

- I have an immense amount of empathy for others and it troubles me greatly when I see anyone who is in distress.

None of which affect my judgement and anyone who has used the word in a negative context to describe me, has always done something wrong and wants to negate responsibility to silence me.

During this particular troublesome time, I sought solace and comfort wherever I could. I had a musical box that played the theme from the film Love Story which my aunt had given me. Inside the box I kept a secret stash of anything that was related to my grandparents: a cigar butt, a serviette, a mint Tic Tac anything that reminded me of them. Nothing was stolen and they were items that would normally have gone into the bin. I used to open the box and have a big old sniff of its contents knowing that it wouldn't be too long before I saw them again. My other stress reliever was to put on some very strange culotte style navy PJs with a lilac belt that were made of super flammable nylon. I decided that I possessed the same martial arts skills as "Hong Kong Phooey" a 70s cartoon. And used to jump off the bunk beds madly kicking around the tiny room. For some strange reason not even known to myself, I found it incredibly cathartic.

I loved a song called "White Horses" by Jacky it was the theme tune to a 1970's children's programme which I couldn't stand. I would listen to the song and then immediately switch the TV off. It was absolutely terrible but not as awful as the Singing Ringing Tree the scariest children's programme ever created. The storyline involved an evil dwarf who stalked a princess and a bear. He would suddenly pop up when you least expected him, especially when the heroine was asleep or vulnerable. As I slept on the top bunk, I convinced myself that he was floating underneath me and would attack me as I slept, check it out on YouTube if you dare!

I invented a discreet and undercover coping mechanism which was deployed immediately after I had been on the receiving end of any verbal abuse. Firstly, I would subtly kick my right leg back as a dog would after doing its business. And then I would turn my back on the offender and perform a second kick and would firmly push the unpleasant waste firmly away from me. For added dramatic effect I would pull a Kenneth Williams style look of disdain. It did help, and I knew that whatever was thrown at me I would eventually be a winner.

When you are a child who is living in an environment that has nothing to offer you by way of nurturing or compassion, the smallest gestures offered by a neglectful parent become magnified. Once mum decided to make Ross and I a cardigan each, and I was asked what colour wool I would like. It was a baseball jacket style design, and I chose a pretty shade of cornflower blue and baby pink, and I was over the moon when I was given it. And on Christmas day she followed an old family tradition of filling a small wooden house with tiny presents that were given out at teatime. I loved that little house and the fact that she had taken the time to wrap up the tiny presents touched me.

Mum always wanted to belong to a group dynamic, and it didn't matter what the ethos of the group was, the weirder the better. For a period of about six months, she got hooked up with the Moonies, and a group of five shiny, happy and very clearly brainwashed individuals besieged the house. I had read an expose in the newspaper at this time about the Moonies, their leader and the finances he was fleecing off his followers as well as the brainwashing tactics they used to recruit people.

I was eleven and onto them and prepared for any brainwashing endeavours they may try on me. Once whilst I was hiding out in my bedroom a French lady entered and told me that she had brought me a gift, a diary and a very odd headscarf. I decided to politely put her straight and tell her that I was off limits and said, " Thank you Marie I really appreciate the thought, it was very kind of you, but I do not want to be a Moonie, so your gift would be wasted on me". A little to the point in hindsight but she kept the gift, and they eventually gave up.

Brigitte loved politics and was a labour councillor, and was extremely proficient and often made valid points. She was no shrinking violet and adored being the centre of attention, it was in all honesty the perfect platform for her.

During my teenage years she became even more self-absorbed and cared only about herself and her latest boyfriend. Ross and I were just unwanted presences in the home which were necessary to receive child benefit and monthly child maintenance from her ex-husband.

One morning when I was walking my usual route to school, I was a little wary because there had been a few rapes in and around the area. Which was a tree lined avenue with large, detached houses that were set about 60 feet back from the pavement. I presumed that the rapist would have been on foot when the crimes were committed, and no one was on foot in the vicinity apart from me. Suddenly a moped came off the road and onto the wide path I was walking on and was trying to knock me to the ground. I began running like I had never run before, with the moped no more than two feet away from me. My loafer shoes came off, and I knew that I could not keep the pace up. If he caught me, I was going to be raped.

Thank goodness a lady in her sixties came out from one of the houses onto the path in front of me and could see that I was being chased and he sped off. To this day I still remember the mopeds registration number. I was in shock and the lady wanted to call the police, but all I could think of was that mum would be angry and I insisted that I would be ok. She knew that I wasn't, and I ran off after thanking her. I met my friend and cried all the way to school

On arrival at school a teacher insisted that she took me home, and she told my mother what had happened and that she needed to call the police immediately, mum said that she would and the teacher left. Brigitte was absolutely furious for being woken up, and told me that she had no intention of calling the police because he hadn't caught me and she couldn't understand why I was making such a fuss about nothing an she went back to bed, this beggar's belief in hindsight.

My brother and I both had insufficient food, and we regularly watched mum and her latest boyfriend tuck into steak and chips. When I started work after leaving Sixth Form, I used to smuggle food in for him, if she had seen it would have been swiftly intercepted. All the food was carbohydrate based as he was way too thin and was kept hidden under his bed.

After their divorce she let loose and quite literally every Tom Dick and Harry were brought back to the house. I am certain that she made as much noise as possible to make us feel sick and uncomfortable. A few of her boyfriends and one-night stands made passes at me, which mum thought amusing, it was an awful environment. Her sister listened to one of mums many "love in's" when she once turned up unannounced. We all sat in the living room waiting for it to stop and she asked my brother and I, " Do you normally hear this"? In unison we replied "yes", but when her sister emerged downstairs, she unsurprisingly said nothing.

I began to have panic attacks and Brigitte seemed to enjoy the fact that I was not coping. During one particularly bad attack I was laying on the settee in a foetal position, whilst she was watching an awful film called The Omega Man starring Charlton Heston. She never normally watched films like it, and I was certain that she had put it on to scare me. I asked her politely if she would change channels as I felt anxious. She refused, smirked and proceeded to tell me that I had lost the plot and needed to see someone.

And so, I made an appointment the following day and saw the most experienced doctor at the practice. I told him that I felt extremely stressed, and was having difficulty sleeping, and that my heart was constantly racing. He listened to my heart and was shocked at just how raised my heartbeat was for a young healthy person. He told me that I could talk to him, and asked me outright "is it your mother"? I just nodded but didn't know where the hell to start, so I didn't attempt to try. Her histrionic episodes had filtered through to the local surgery as she had created a fuss in there a few times, her reputation usually preceded her. He quite rightly gave me propranolol a beta blocker to slow down my elevated heart rate. Which I did try but it made me feel a little lightheaded and far too aware of my heart which freaked me out.

One of her attentions seeking routines that used to seriously wind me up. Was ringing The Samaritans and telling them a pack of lies. She used to do the hyperventilating routine and wailed like a banshee in between each dramatic breath. It was all part of the narcissist and histrionic DSM which I was to learn about much later. On one occasion she had gone into the premises where they were based, in clear need of some concentrated one on one narcissistic supply. It was at the time when I was having severe anxiety attacks, working full time and I was exhausted. It was the weekend, and I received a phone call from them telling me that I needed to pick her up as she was very distressed and could not be left alone. I walked on auto pilot the couple of miles to the house where they were based, and rang the doorbell a lady answered, and I walked in. She must have thought that I was the most heartless daughter in the world because I just ignored her. Whilst she relayed her great concerns about my mum's mental welfare. She had been completely suckered in. I thought you haven't got a clue, what you see is not remotely the truth. It was me who needed some support and not my drama addicted mother.

Around this time, I met my first boyfriend Seb in the local pub. Mum was seeing one of her on off boyfriends, who had dumped her again. She wanted to confront him and did not want to go alone, and so to keep the peace I went. He was five years older than me, and we began chatting and got on well.

When we first began dating, mum was not in the least bit happy. It was my day off work and at dinner time Brigitte surfaced from her boudoir and came downstairs. And began screaming at me yelling "How dare I sit there and look so happy and calm"? to which I responded that I was just watching telly and I didn't want any trouble. Suddenly she launched herself at me and began pulling my hair, in between slapping and scratching my face. I stood up and managed to push her off me, and she fell into a dramatic heap on the floor. Going immediately into victim mode she told me that she was going to call the police. I replied, "you do that mum I would welcome it, and I will tell them precisely what led me to push you over". Of course, she didn't call them because she knew that the truth would out, she never attacked me again physically after that.

I felt it far too dangerous to stay in the house and fled round to Seb's who lived on the same estate. He was still at work, and his mum answered the door. She was such a sweet lady, very no nonsense but extremely kind. She took one look at my face and said that I needed to call the police. there were scratch marks, swelling and redness on both of my cheeks. She said that if I didn't, I was not allowed to go back to the house, and so I stayed with them for two weeks.

One day she was in the local mini market and the cashier was telling someone in the queue what an old slapper my mum was, and that as I was living with her the apple didn't fall far from the tree. In front of a shop full of people she told the cashier that her comments about my mother were indeed accurate, but she would not tolerate people speaking about me in the same terms as I was my mother's opposite, and she made the lady apologise which was so kind of her,

Seb and I dated for three years and I got married when I was 19. I was far too young, and on my wedding day I felt so sad and guilty, as I knew that I was making a big mistake. I liked him very much and didn't want to hurt him, and I hoped that one day that I would feel the same for him as he did for me. Two years later I had our daughter Faye, who was the most wonderful of blessings.

Not long after her arrival mum hooked up and married a much younger man, and left the Country without so much as a backwards glance. A few months later she announced that she was pregnant and told me that as I had a baby, she thought she would have one too. Hardly a sensible reason for a 43-year-old woman to have a child but nothing ever did make any sense.

For a few years all was peaceful and quiet on the western front as the flights were extremely expensive. She came back about three times in total in an eleven-year period. The first time she came with my half-brother, and they stayed with us for ten days. We were all looking forward to seeing him, but Seb and I were not overly enamoured at the prospect of her staying with us. We knew only too well from experience that we would be walking on eggshells the entire time and constantly firefighting to keep the house peaceful. However, we knew that there was no other option, my grandparents were too old to play hosts and they also had a smaller house. Faye was just over three years old, and my half-brother just over two.

 I was determined that during their stay the two children would have as nice a time as possible, and luckily, she only kicked off once which wasn't bad going. Faye and my half-brother had been playing and out of the blue he ran up to her and grabbed hold of her cheeks, squeezing and nipping them with a great deal of force. Faye was shocked and burst into tears. I immediately told him calmly but firmly that he must not do things like that as it had hurt Faye who was only little like him. I wasn't in the least bit angry, but he needed to be told. Mum was in the room and had seen what had happened and was furious that I had gently corrected her son. She informed me that it was her job to do so if she thought it necessary and he was only playing. I did not consider scratching and nipping normal play. I immediately recalled the crescent shaped nail marks which were often on my wrists as a child. I wondered whether my brother had seen this behaviour, and he was mimicking it which worried me. Faye had very red cheeks and a couple of scratches on them, and I said to mum " You need to gently correct your son, he has hurt Faye and if you don't tell him its wrong, he will do it to other children".

She then became extremely nasty and decided to project the blame onto me and called Faye a spoilt stupid little bitch. Although Faye was an only child she was never spoiled as I wanted her to have a balanced childhood as I knew only too well the importance of stability. Yes, I made mistakes as all parents do but spoiling her was not one of them. How I came down from that one in hindsight I truly do not know. To be honest if my brother had not been part of the equation, I would have told her to leave, but I was caught between a rock and a hard place.

One day mum went out on her own to meet an old friend, so we were able to completely relax and do precisely what we wanted. I often sing and dance and generally love acting like a big kid, so I joined in and played with them both. It was important to me that we all had at least one private happy memory. I put on an 80's compilation album which had The Stranglers hit Heroes on. My little brother loved the track and asked for it to be played repeatedly, he was dancing and trying to sing along in a manly voice, it was such a sweet memory bless him.

I did notice however that developmentally something was amiss, I had to very actively make him engage with me and his surroundings. I thought he had a hearing problem at first, so when Brigitte wasn't about, I made noises like clapping, clicking my fingers whistling etc. And each time he turned his head towards the sound, so it clearly was not a hearing issue.

He had brought some little toy cars over with him and I noticed that he was completely lost in the routine of lining them up in a certain way. I then thought it was potentially something on the autistic spectrum, but I didn't know what as he did engage at times very well. After they had left and flown home, I stupidly told my aunt that I was a little worried about him, I said he was adorable but there was something slightly amiss. An extremely bad move as she proceeded to give me a lecture. She told me that I was being ridiculous, and he was extremely sweet and there was nothing at all wrong with him. I agreed that he was sweet, but it wasn't regarding his appearance or character. And about a child having a problem assessed early, so that developmentally they could reach their full potential. My aunt has no children through choice and has rarely spent any time around youngsters but her hellbent determination to override me, stopped any chance of a logical discussion.

About three weeks after Brigitte and my brother had returned home, I turned on the telly to watch my weekly episode of Panorama, and low and behold it was dedicated to something called Aspergers which I had never heard of. I watched intently and listened to parents discussing their children's problems. How they behaved and interacted with others, and it was a clear match as to how my little brother had behaved throughout his stay. It wasn't an ideal situation but the sooner it was recognized the better it would be for him in the long run.

Brigitte used to ring once a fortnight and would talk about herself whilst I listened as per usual. I still don't know how I managed to do this, but during the call I interrupted her. And calmly told her that I thought her son was beautiful and I was not implying that she was a neglectful mother as she was doing a fantastic job. However, I had seen a programme about something called Aspergers and it wasn't anything to worry about, but maybe she would consider taking him to the doctors. She didn't kick up a fuss and listened to me, I cannot tell you how surprised and relieved I was. A couple of days later she took him to the doctors who subsequently made an appointment for him at a famous Children's hospital, and it was confirmed that he did indeed have Aspergers.

After a few years of peace and quiet all hell was let loose abroad, a custody battle involving a restraining order with regards to domestic abuse had been breached. She told me her ex had breached the order, however I found out years later that the order was taken against her, and she had been sent to prison for a few days. She had decided to return to the UK and none of us could cope with the prospect.

During this time Brigitte had divulged to my aunt that she had been forced to have a psychological appraisal during the court case and was beside herself. My aunt told me this during a phone conversation. Mum had told her that this bloody awful woman had told her that she had something called narcissistic personality disorder. We discussed it at great length, and I told her that I didn't know what it was, but I would research it. I was intrigued but also relieved, finally there was a name to what I had always known, something had always been very wrong with her. I subsequently researched NPD with regards to mum and all necessary criteria was a DSM match. She was in no doubt a malignant narcissist, but at the time there was little said about the damage it causes their children, all of them whether the golden child or the scapegoat.

My aunt does not recall this conversation at all and when I mentioned it several years later. She told me that she didn't know or have a clue what I was talking about, and that she had never said such a thing and where the hell was, I getting this stupid information from? It was crazy and was most definitely a spot of gaslighting, but I had no clue as to why she would do this.

There is without doubt a clear genetic predisposition towards mental health problems within my family, there is a strong underlying theme and consistency with regards to certain traits. I have been very lucky, as it has bypassed both me and my daughter. Of course, I have many faults and without doubt I have inherited some unhealthy psychological "fleas" which are not ideal. I wonder sometimes whether the sensitive side of my personality is a result of my childhood environment and part of a coping mechanism. But long before it had begun to take a toll on me, I was quiet, often lost in deep thought and I wanted everyone to be happy.

Song: Angels by Robbie Williams

ROOM 6

Guilt

And now onto an off load about "False Memory Syndrome" with regards to the death of a close family member. Not surprisingly it occurred within my family and without doubt millions of others have experienced precisely the same.

You should treat every person that you love, like it's their very last day, if you love them tell them, show them, there may not be another day to prove it. I doubt that this will apply to anyone who is reading this who is on the same page as me, but for anyone who has been too busy to see someone whom they profess to love, pull your finger out now and do something about it before it's too late. Rewriting history may temporarily assuage personal guilt, but a conscience that relates to facts will eventually surface, and niggle away at the soul unless it is completely seared.

I considered my grandparents to be my parents and the feeling was mutual. They referred to me as their third daughter, Seb as their son in law and Faye as their granddaughter. As a young adult I continued to see them regularly, and when I got married, we all spent almost every Sunday in their company right up until their deaths. We had many lovely days spent with them, and never once had so much as a cross word or an argument. Seb used to cut the grass for them, and we once decorated the living room and laid a new carpet when they had gone away on holiday. Gran had been nagging grandad about it and they were over the moon to return home to a mini makeover.

My aunt was a career woman, and she visited them at max three times a year. However, her mum loved her a great deal and very much looked forward to her visits. I found the relationship to be a little one sided and based very much on her daughter turning up with gifts and taking her out on trips. Throughout her life she lived at least four hours away from her parents, and it felt to me like the mileage was a safety buffer and an excuse for her to only go when it suited her. There were issues between her, and her father and her visits often stressed him out. He was not perfect and was admittedly a little complex at times, but he was a very kind, gentle and deep man. He once told me that she never tried to understand him and the only way she was able to show any affection was by giving gifts or money.

My brother Ross also saw them very infrequently, around two to three times a year. At one point he was stationed two miles away from them, and I gently suggested that it may be an idea if he visited them a little more often, because they loved him very much. He replied, "You just don't understand how busy I am Kim", and he didn't take me up on my gently worded suggestion. He clearly thought that there was always tomorrow and that they were immortal, but of course none of us are.

Luckily, they were extremely independent and, on the ball, pretty much to the end, but on a few occasions Seb and I stepped in. They were both extremely proud, so we kept a loving but very discreet eye on them. One such occasion was a couple of years prior to my grandad passing, I had rung gran and although she was talking normally, I felt something was amiss. We hadn't been for our usual Sunday visit as we all had heavy colds, and it had been nearly a fortnight since we had seen them. After the phone call I got straight on the next train to see what was wrong. On arrival gran met me at the door and looked terrible and promptly burst into tears. I asked her what was the matter and where was grandad. She proceeded to tell me that he had been in bed for a week and had told her that he was tired of living and being in an old and failing body. She had tried absolutely everything to get him up and did not know what to do.

I wasn't sure either as when he had decided a course of action like me, he was as stubborn as hell. I went into his room, and he looked dreadful, deathly pale and had lost a great deal of weight. He was unshaven and his normally neat silver hair was unkempt. I did something that I would never normally do, I shouted at him, as drastic measures were called for. I asked him what the hell he thought he was doing, and for someone who had fought in the war and was my role model, he was behaving like a pathetic coward. To lay there and to decide to die was not the order of things, it was for God to decide when it was his time and not him.

I told him that his wife was outside heartbroken, and he needed to get his sorry backside off that bed himself, or I would pull him up. He smiled at me so beautifully and said, "Well my Mishka, I haven't got much option have I, I better get my sorry arse up, can you give me a hand"?

They gave so much to me throughout their lives, and it was our absolute pleasure to be around them, they were so interesting and terribly dignified and they deserved their last few months to be quiet and peaceful, sadly not to be...

Due to their dreadful last Christmas in 1998 which was one of my mother's best and most memorable rage filled narcissistic histrionic routines. Which has been completely swept under the carpet to suit. Grandad although old was very peaceful leading up to this event, realistically he was winding down, but I strongly believe that the stress acted as a catalyst and brought his life to an end quicker than it was meant, he completely gave up.

Although my grandparents were very resilient, the odds of both of them surviving another year were rapidly decreasing. I spoke to mum once a fortnight and when she asked about their health and general wellbeing, I always told her the truth. Regardless of my strained relationship with her, they were her parents. It was highly probable that it would be the last Christmas that they would both see their first-born child and their youngest grandchild. I told her that realistically time was not infinite, and she decided to fly over. It was the golden opportunity for her to leave them with some happy memories, and I foolishly thought that it would be the case. She came over with my brother a few days before Christmas and it was planned that we would go with Ross to see them on Boxing Day.

On arrival at their house sadly it was clear from the offset that her expectations were based solely on her being the star attraction of the entire day. The dynamic immediately felt uncomfortable and strained which would have been manageable, if there had been no trigger factors to enrage her. Villain, victim or heroine it never did matter, attention was what she always sought and one way or another she always managed to achieve her goal. After an hour of relative peace gran and I laid out the table for dinner, a Boxing Day buffet of cold turkey, salad and baked potatoes finished off with a sherry trifle.

Unfortunately, my youngest brother began touching all of the baked potatoes in the basket and was searching for the largest for himself. I did not blame him in the least, it was not an Aspergers trait, and was simply because he had never been corrected or told what acceptable and polite behaviour was. Ross was watching and not impressed he politely said to mum " Can you please stop him doing that, it's unhygienic and we all have to eat, he is the youngest and shouldn't have the largest of anything". Ross was right of course but this innocent remark was all that was needed, mum had finally been given her trigger, and she was eager to pull it and fire off more than a few rounds.

Instead of replying to Ross, she spun round to me and launched a personal attack. She screamed "Who the hell do you think you are, standing there like that, you make me bloody sick, and you always have?". I quietly and calmly replied that I had not said a word which infuriated her, and she called me a "Stupid little bitch". I remained calm and told her that I didn't like Faye hearing raised voices, and that it was inappropriate behaving like this in front of her aging parents who were used to peace and quiet. Seb stepped in also and told her that her behaviour was completely inappropriate and unfair. However, she still carried on with her banshee style attack, it was relentless. I decided it was best not to respond, as I knew that it would make an inflammatory situation far worse. I sat down on my gran's favourite prayer chair, which as a child I loved and hoped that perhaps some divine intervention would come into play. However, none was forthcoming, and I began to tremble a little.

Gran pleaded with her to stop and asked why she was screaming at me as I had done nothing wrong. And at this point grandad stepped in and walked up to mum looking far younger than he had done for years. He raised his arthritic hand which was normally in a position of semi closure. And the determination was written all over his face and this had clearly transferred directly to his hand which miraculously became fully opened and flat. He pulled his arm back ready to slap her face, whilst looking at her with the utmost disdain he said, "You absolutely disgust me, but I will not dirty my hand you are not worth it", he then dropped his hand back down to his side. Mum carried on oblivious to reality and was alternating between screaming obscenities, hyperventilating and professing victimhood.

Ross walked over to me and said, "Come on sis I need to get you out of here, let's go to the beach for a walk". I looked across at Seb and he said he would keep an eye on my grandparents and little brother, and we left. Not long after Seb also left and took Faye home.

There was no way Brigitte could have come back to our home after how she had behaved. And she and her son stayed the last night of her holiday with her parents, which worried me a great deal. Before they left for home they met up with my aunt at a local park. Faye decided that she would like to go, not to see mum again but she felt dreadfully sorry for my half-brother as did I.

When she returned home, she told me that mum had been convincing her sister that she had done nothing wrong and had been the victim. And naturally I had been assigned the lead role of evil villain in the never-ending family drama.

Faye proudly told me that she had stood it for only for so long, but then had to put the record straight. She told her great aunt that her grandmother was lying and all that she was telling her was completely untrue. I thank God that it was in a public place I was so proud of her. It had taken a terrible toll on us all, I knew that the emotional damage inflicted on my grandparents was never going to be healed, time was not on their side.

Two weeks later grandad told me that he was going to die shortly, and I sadly knew that he was telling the truth. The spark had gone from his knowing blue eyes and there was nothing that I could do or say to bring that twinkle back. He took me for a drink in his local pub and we had a heart to heart. We discussed the dreadful Boxing Day episode, and sadly he said "I have tried all my life to try and save that woman, she cannot be saved, and I never wish to see her again as long as I live" he was heartbroken. It was awful to see a man with such a strong faith lose hope. I also had decided that I no longer wanted anything to do with her and told him so. He understood completely and said there was no need for me to explain. We were united in our position and had both reached the point of no return.

He told me how proud he was of me, and that he and gran had tried extremely hard to adopt me. But mum had told them if they did that, they would never see Ross again and nor would I. He said he was sorry that he couldn't protect me as much as he had wanted to, but he and gran had done all that they could for me. I thanked him and reassured him that they could have not done anything more, and that they had been my rocks. He went on to tell me that he felt it was very important that I had someone strong in my corner, as he was concerned that some people did not have my best interests at heart.

This I picked up on, as he clearly used the word "some" and the only other person that would fit the brief along with mum was my aunt. I wondered what he had heard over the years and whether there had been family arguments, in relation to my childhood and the care and attention that they had both given me. He told me I needed to find my real dad, who although he had only met briefly, he didn't think was a bad person. He said that he had been furious with him when he left mum in the family way, but in hindsight he was just a young man who had been "sowing far too many wild oats". I promised him that I would try and do so at some point in the future but not then, because I considered him to be my father in every true sense of the word.

He thanked me for the extra two years he had lived after I had given him "a serious telling off", which with the exception of Christmas had been peaceful. He told me that I was right, and it wasn't his time to die then, but it was now. And I must accept it and to always remember that he loved me very much. It was only "his suit" that would disappear, and he would keep an eye on me always.

Before he was admitted to hospital, he had been bedridden for a few days and called me to his room. He asked me to open the top drawer of his chest of drawers and to look for a small brown leather box, I did so and handed it to him. He told me that it contained something very dear to him and he wanted to ensure that he gave it to me personally before he died. He said only gran and I would appreciate the sentimental value of it, and he did not want anyone else owning it when he passed. It was his mother's gold portrait broach with a photo of him inside when he was a toddler. I was honoured that he gave it to me, and I treasure it.

True to his word a couple of days later he was hospitalized and gradually slipped away over a period of approximately three weeks. While he was in the last couple of weeks of his life, my aunt came up to stay with her mum for a couple of days to support her. She popped round to our house unexpectedly and announced that she was leaving and returning home as "Father is making it up and is not as ill as he is claiming to be". I could not believe what I was hearing, she said it haughtily and with absolute conviction. I quietly replied," please don't go, you will never see him alive again if you do". I said this solely for her benefit so she could spend a little time with him, I knew she was making a very big mistake, but she ignored me and left.

I went with gran to see him on what turned out to be his last day. He was terribly dignified and had what seemed to be a dialysis line positioned in his neck, his kidneys must have been shutting down. I stroked his head with my thumb just as he had done mine when I needed him, and I told him that I loved him very much. Gran was rooted to the spot with grief and hardly spoke it was awful. He told me " Please take your gran away now" he wanted to die alone, and I understood that completely, But I asked a nurse if she would hold his hand at the end which she assured me she would. I sat with gran in their house for the news that he had passed. There was nothing to say, and I comforted her as best I could, she was heartbroken as was I.

Mum could not attend his funeral as she had only just returned home, and my aunt did not believe just how serious and damaging the situation had been for us all. She naturally was aligned with her sister in their shared grief, which I understood but the whole narrative had little to no bearing on facts. When the coffin left their house, my aunt was snapping shots of it for her sister in a manner that was obvious to all, and I felt in terribly poor taste, discreet was nowhere in the equation. It felt like a blinking circus and her husband Robert voiced precisely what I was thinking.

However, his funeral was very dignified and befitting of a true gentleman and more people attended than I expected. There was an RAF base located a couple of miles away, and as luck would have it during the service a roar of tornado engines went directly overhead, which he would have loved. The eulogy however was a different matter, apart from grans input with regards to her own personal memories of her dear late husband, it had been hijacked into a load of gushy and quite frankly guilt-ridden hypocrisy. Halfway through it gran turned to me and shook her head and said, "Kim this is so wrong, he loved you and your little family so much". I gently touched her forearm and said, "Please don't worry about it, you know that, and so did we and that's all that matters". My aunt had not mentioned the eulogy to me and had asked Ross to write it, with I suspect a great deal of input from her.

There was a tale about mums last meal out with them both, which was an absolute load of flowery tosh which finished with "Fly high father with your beautiful wings". My aunt had a similarly wonderful tale of devotion, memories and love. We got a tiny mention at the very end simply stating that he had three beloved grandchildren and a great granddaughter. Even poor Ross who had helped write it was not permitted a personal mention, it was quite frankly a joke. I know that there are probably many of you out there that have experienced the same. It is very hurtful when history is changed to suit and is adapted to suit personal agendas.

His wake was held in his favourite watering hole, I went in and ordered verbatim his regular "half a pint of Adnams in a glass with a handle please". We sat quietly for a while and then it began, my aunts very loud memory monologue. Telling all within a 30 feet radius, what she had done for him, her cherished memories, and the special relationship that she had with them both. Along with the consistent support she had given them throughout the years, you name it she had done it. I knew that she had helped grandad out financially a few times which was good of her. But there was little forthcoming with regards to anything else. Then Ross decided to join in, and it was getting louder and louder, I was stuck in the middle of a sound surround system which I could not bear. I found it awful and inappropriate as gran sat in numbed, grief-stricken silence. I pretended that I needed the loo and went to a different area of the hotel to compose myself. Suddenly James the vicar who I had not seen for years, walked over to me and gently placed his hand on my shoulder, and said " I see this so much in my line of work, those who make the most noise have the most guilt. I know precisely just how much your grandparents love you and how much you and your family love them" he smiled so sweetly at me and walked away. There is nothing wrong with being quiet, I am glad that I am as empty vessels often do make the most noise.

Gran passed away three months later from pneumonia, I knew that she wanted to be with her husband and was absolutely lost without him. I visited her with my aunt and the last time she spoke to me I was at the foot of her bed. She was on a high dose of diamorphine and very calm. My aunt was by her side, and she asked her "Where is my Mishka"? I replied, "I'm here gran" and went over to her. She said, "We are on a boat Mishka" to which I replied," I know we are gran isn't it lovely"? She passed away a couple of days later peacefully in her sleep, bless her dear little heart.

We have no second chances, please tell all the special people in your life that you love them and actually back up your words with actions. Do not live in denial or guilt it's not healthy, make your memories count and make them reality based.

Songs:

Life's What You Make It by Talk Talk

The Living Years by Mike and The Mechanics

While My Guitar Gently Weeps by George Harrison

ROOM 7

The Smirk

After my grandparent's death Brigitte returned to the Country after the break down of her marriage. I was still not in contact with her, and I felt a lot calmer not having her in my life. But with the benefit of hindsight, I do not believe I had fully severed the ties, or truly dealt with all the emotions that needed to be processed to achieve the permanent stance of No Contact.

My aunt remained in contact with her and told me that she had come back to the Country after her divorce. And had moved back to the area that I lived, which was not in the least ideal. I had to be extremely careful when I went out shopping or to a local public venue. I did see her a few times whilst out and about but always managed to avoid physically bumping into her. And it remained the case for several years until I made a very big error of judgement.

I was struggling with a situation at home, and I no longer had a matriarchal figure to turn to for advice. I rarely seek help or support from anyone and always try to carry my own water. However, I was desperately in need of some advice and rung my aunt to discuss my dilemma. Although I had listened to her on many occasions and helped her a great deal practically after my grandparent's death, it was not reciprocal. It was the first time I had ever sought advice from her, and she dismissed me pretty much immediately. She told me that my mother was the person that I should talk to about my problem and not her. She gave me her phone number and told me to get back in touch with her. Mum was the last person I should have spoken to with regards to the situation in which I had found myself in. I wonder in hindsight whether that was why my aunt passed the buck, as it made life and the situation far more complicated for me and also her sister.

I should have slept on the problem and given myself some time to calm down but foolishly I didn't. And that very same evening I dialled the number my aunt had given me and spoke to mum. Although I felt awkward when talking to her oddly enough, she spoke to me as if there had been no gap in our communication. To explain my problem, I had to disclose some information that involved her. Although I was very tearful during the call I was diplomatic, empathetic and considerate in my wording when I told her about my recent discovery, and the problem that had arisen from it. She was surprisingly calm throughout and told me to come round and see her and I did.

For a few visits all was ok and she was surprisingly pleasant and seemed far less self-absorbed. Ever the optimist I thought that age had mellowed her, and I hoped that we would have a healthier mother and daughter relationship. But with the benefit of hindsight; she was being on her best behaviour for a reason. By having me back in her life there was a possibility of her somehow benefiting from the situation which I had discussed with her. When she realized that it was extremely unlikely that this would happen and there was nothing in it for her, over the next six months her mask began to gradually slip. I would have loved for a happy ending to our story but when narcissism is in the relationship dynamic you have to adopt one of two approaches. You can stay in the relationship by accepting the disorder and keeping yourself very safe, or you leave.

Sadly, all of her previous negative and manipulative behavioural traits were once more very apparent. I would have left the situation sooner, but there now was something else in the dynamic who had to be considered, my younger half- brother.

When I got back in touch with mum many years had passed, and my youngest brother was thirteen. I got on very well with him and although we hadn't spent time together, I felt very protective of him. The brother and sister connection was there without having to put in any effort. He was a gentle giant, socially awkward but considerate and kind. I watched the way mum interacted with him and although he was the newly appointed Golden Child, it was very clear that he was not receiving guidance and input which would help him cope in the wider world.

He was micro- managed on many levels, ignored in others and she infantilized him. I felt that she used his condition to keep him firmly in the role of controlled Golden Child. She could purvey to the world that she was a saintly mother who coped incredibly well with her son and his condition. The relationship dynamic was very insular, and he needed to have some healthy third-party input. Which would encourage him to show others that he was an autonomous individual who was more than capable of making decisions independently of his mother.

With regards to his father who still lived abroad he had been fed a very negative narrative. His father was clearly not perfect, but the way mum spoke about him he was the devil incarnate. It was a clear case of parental alienation, a tactic that narcissists employ to control the narrative a child has about their absent parent. By giving a false one it enables them to maintain complete unchallenged control of the child. With absolutely no thought or consideration that the child may benefit from having the other parent in their lives.

My aunt was in his life and he was taken on holidays with them both and she would take him out for treats. All very material and very much the same dynamic as with her parents. A distant and seemingly loving relationship, but with very little inter- personal effort.

My brother Ross used to try and give some input and occasionally he managed to have some alone time with his brother. However, mum actively discouraged this and told me that she didn't like them having time together when she was not present. Although Ross was The Golden Child as a boy, his teenage years had left him in no doubt that mum was unpleasant, neglectful and cruel. And unlike me he was very vocal about his thoughts, and used to tell her to her face as well as others. Although what he said was true, his situation had not been as bad as mine and his main gripe was about the poor food and dirty conditions in the home. It wasn't healthy him remaining in her life and vice versa, and he did so from a distance. He would turn up occasionally and have a go at her, and the next visit he would ask for help and be the caring and thoughtful son. Ross was the unknown quantity with mum as she couldn't control his moods, words or the narrative that she had set, and this unsettled her.

As a young child Ross never sat still and couldn't concentrate wherever he was you knew about it. He was annoying but I loved him very much and felt protective of him particularly when he entered his teens. He seemed to be troubled and was either hyper and mischievous or very quiet and looked very sad. As soon as he was an adult, he left home to join the

RAF and I understood why. We didn't speak on the phone very often and tended to meet up in person. I have always been a steady eddy unless something awful has happened, my personality on a daily basis is consistent. Boring perhaps, but it is constant on all levels: my opinions, speech and sense of humour have never changed and unless I am unfortunate and get an illness that affects my cognitive abilities, they never will.

Ross sadly was very different and has been mentally fragile throughout his entire adult life. He rapid cycles between normal regular moods, bouts of severe depression and then to manic high episodes in which he has superhero status. Reality goes completely out the window, and he is super loud and talks very rapidly, which I am in no doubt is bipolar. This has caused him difficulty with regards to holding down relationships and also at work, which is so sad because he is a good-hearted man, but unwell.

As far as I am aware he never has got treatment and when he is down, he will attribute his mental state to a physical problem, which was often magnified out of proportion or self-diagnosed. When we used to meet up in the main, we had good times, because when he was depressed, he used to hole himself up in his home for months and I never saw him. We rarely rowed and the only time we butted heads is when I stood up to him when he was being nonsensical. Or I told him a gentle truth that he needed to hear for his own wellbeing. So, for very different reasons than mum, I also was a little concerned about him giving our youngest sibling input that may be unhealthy. Ross would never knowingly do the wrong thing, but unfortunately sometimes he isn't in the right headspace to make a correct judgement call.

As I was the only third party in the mix that could truly give my youngest brother sound advice and I was very fond of him. I could not leave him alone to deal with a situation that he considered to be the norm when it clearly was not. Although mum was always with us, we had some good times together and for a while my decision to stay in the dynamic was not tested...

Until one afternoon I went round to see them, and all hell was kicking off. My brother had been arguing with her and was not playing ball. On my arrival she immediately began her histrionic routine and began to hyperventilate. This saddened me, because regardless of my brother's favourite status, he was without doubt witnessing the same as I did as a child. I went with him into his room and sat down on his bed, I held his hand and told him not to worry. And blow me down, we listened to her whilst she made a call to The Samaritans. Informing them of how unkind and cruel her children were, and a load of old rubbish about her tragic life.

Once she had offloaded all her fake woes onto the poor recipient of the call. I turned to my brother and said, "I am so sorry, I have heard this once too often, this is nothing to do with you, but I am not going to stand for this any longer". I went into the living room and told my mother in no uncertain terms what I thought of her. Which was that she was a terrible mother, who lied and manipulated to meet her own ends. And that when she was diagnosed as a narcissist the psychologist was bang on, and she was as mad as a box of frogs. I wanted nothing more to do with her, and I meant every single long overdue word.

I grabbed my coat and walked towards my car, with her following and screaming obscenities, which I didn't respond to. I had no intention of ever seeing her again as long as I lived, but suddenly my poor teenage brother came out and was extremely distressed. He was running up and down the street with his arms flailing. Because of his Aspergers his co-ordination was incredibly clumsy, and it broke my heart. I went back because I felt like I was deserting him, and I could not do it.

During this time, she was the central communication point of the remaining family, and there was without a shadow of a doubt a triangulation dynamic regarding conversations, face to face or on the phone. To put it bluntly she held court and shit stirred for England. As we were not in each other's pockets

24/7 to clarify facts, I am sure that an awful lot of lies were told to keep us separate, a strong element of "divide and conquer" was at play.

One of our last family gatherings was we attended a carol service. Whilst walking back after the service to the car, Faye, my youngest brother and I, were briskly walking upfront. All trying to avoid as much conversation with mum and her sister as possible. Suddenly my aunt sidled up behind us and declared "Isn't Ross doing well with his business, I am so proud of him"? He had just been declared bankrupt and was struggling with his mental health at the time. I asked "Where she had got that information from, as he was really struggling and just been declared bankrupt" she replied "Your mother", which was her "go to" when she decides her relationship with her sister could actually be a little iffy, and wants to put the onus and ownership of a problem firmly at my doorstep.

I managed to stay in my youngest brother and Brigittes lives as long as I could. I grey rocked a lot of the time and if I could see that it wasn't working, I used to flatter her ego by complimenting her on something or other that she had done. I used to listen to hours of her talking about herself and the tragic life that she had led. She often used to say that there should be a film made about her. I wonder what that would have been about, clearly not Mommie Dearest, or Postcards from the Edge! I am sure she was thinking a narrative along the lines of Joan of Arc, with a beautiful actress such as Angelina Jolie playing the lead role. I was not being myself at all around her, I was simply keeping safe. However, it did not overly affect me, as once I understand a dynamic, I can cope with it. The straw that broke the camel's back was something little and, in all honesty, simply a "look" she gave me.

I had decided to move to a different part of the country and had got a reasonable job in a hospital. I had not ventured out of my home County my entire life and felt it was time for me to "grow a pair" and do something a little different. Just before I moved, I had a sad but sweet conversation with my younger brother which was extremely telling. When I had gone to see them, mum was out, and after letting me in he told me to sit down because he needed to discuss something very serious with me. I sat and listened while he proceeded to tell me that mum was extremely upset and felt very betrayed that I was moving away, after all the sacrifices love and care she had given me as a child.

A little awkward to say the least and I did not want to burst his bubble it would not have been appropriate or fair. So, I explained to him that life can be interpreted differently by individuals and my take was not entirely the same. His mum loved him very much and that was all he should ever worry about. The sound of an ice-cream van blasting out "Just One Cornetto" broke the awkward moment, and he jumped up and said, "Sorry Kim, I didn't want to upset you let me buy you an ice cream" and off he went. This has brought tears to my eyes, a very sweet lad.

Soon after our conversation he went to university to study for a PHD. He was very gifted in one particular subject, and I knew without a shadow of a doubt that he would achieve his goal. Mum still was very much a part of his life whilst he was away, clearly too much so. Of course, he did need a little extra support and input because of his Aspergers, but she was overly controlling even from a distance. He once had a girlfriend who was from Iran and mum didn't trust her. She decided that the young woman was a foreign spy who had specifically targeted her son because of his trusting nature. Apparently, she was planning to extricate information from him about his chosen subject which could have security implications for the Country. She told me that she and her sister thought the same and they were all primed up to rescue him from her evil clutches and implement a deprogramming regime!

I moved away and saw her a few more times, and the final visit I stayed with her, which was not overly wise, but I believe everything happens for a reason...

Unbeknownst to me this also was the last time I was to see Ross. He came round to see me at mums and looked a little troubled and depressed. But we were both very pleased to see each other and hugged each other tightly. As Ross wouldn't eat anything that mum cooked, I gave her some money to buy us fish and chips. She went to get them and we chatted about all that we had done since we had last spoken.

The past few days that I had spent at mums had been stressful, and Ross suspected as much. I told him it had been difficult, but I was going home in a couple of days' time and that I just wanted to keep the peace. I admitted she was as bad as ever and he agreed that she was. He gave me another hug and told me that I should have stayed with him. But I hadn't wanted to because the last time we had spoken, he had rung me on a manic high and was making little to no sense and was very overbearing. We ate our fish supper and he only stayed for about forty minutes after we had finished eating. It was clear that he was not in the mood to be around her for very long. We hugged once more and he said, look after yourself sis" to which I replied, " you too" and he left.

The following day whilst we were having a cuppa Brigitte began one of her drawn out me, me and a bit more me monologues, about various subjects all of which I had heard a million times before. And then she suddenly changed tack; and began to go on and on about her parents and how much she missed them. The huge part that they had played in her life, and all that she had done for them, all of which was untrue. She was on a roll and would not stop and said that the loss was almost unbearable for her, her sister, both her sons, the milkman, her cat etc. It was relentless and she kept mentioning herself, her sister and two sons in an exclusive group that were united in their grief and also in their acts of kindness. Although logic and facts should have given me comfort, I knew that she was goading me. After listening for around fifteen minutes, I could feel tears of frustration trickle down my cheek. I wanted to scream at her that she had broken her father's heart and that the pain I had seen in her mother's eyes after Boxing Day was all down to her, but it would have been pointless.

I averted my gaze and looked for something to focus on rather than her, I chose the coffee table which had loads of little dusty white cherubs scattered all over it. After months of wondering just how many were occupying the space, I decided to count them and when I had reached the final tally of fourteen. I looked up once more at her whilst she was still speaking and was shocked to the core by the look on her face. One I will never forget, akin to a murderer after a kill: gleeful, triumphant, gloating and that blinking smirk was written all over her smug face.

I casually wiped my tears away and rapidly changed the subject; I made out I was ok as I knew I was going home the following morning. I told her that I had a headache and retired to bed early and cried quietly into my pillow. I stayed awake all night with her cat sleeping beside me, he gave me comfort and stopped me from leaving in the middle of the night.

I kept looking at my watch and managed to lay there until 7.30 a.m. I was on auto pilot talking and remaining polite, but my heart had finally closed to her at the ripe old age of 48. I thanked her for letting me stay and told her that I would be leaving early as it was a long drive home. I wished her a Happy Mother's Day which was in two days' time and told her that I had left her present on the coffee table. I looked at her and smiled and knew without a shadow of a doubt that I would never see her again.

I knew that for me to properly understand all that had happened and to remain mentally healthy I was going to have to research the family dynamic of a narcissist mother, rather than just understand the DSM criteria that she fulfilled. I was very upset but pretty much got onto it straight away. Between feeling shocked and bouts of crying I read things online and brought a book called "You're Not Crazy it's your Mother" by Danu Morrigan. It was the simple and to the point title that made me buy it. Although it was a brief read and simply written, many of the incidents that the author described were the same as mine. I felt relieved that it was clearly a modus operandi that all narcissistic mothers used, and there were millions of people like me in the same boat. I decided to research a lot more about it, learn, understand grieve, cry, heal and eventually move on. During the week after I had returned home, she tried to call me a few times. Which was unusual as we normally spoke once every seven to ten days unless I had a dramatic voicemail to contact her urgently about her latest crisis. I was in no doubt that she knew that something was wrong, but I ignored the calls. Because I was the scapegoat, I knew that more than likely she would not bother with me too much, if I had been the Golden Child, it would have been a very different story.

An explanation for my decision was not necessary but I gave her one as recommended by "You're Not Crazy" simply so I could have closure and she would know there was no going back. I wrote her a brief note addressing her by her Christian name and I thanked her for having me, I briefly explained that I felt our relationship was not healthy, and it was no longer good for me to be around her. I wished her health, peace and happiness for the future and I meant it.

My aunt and brother both knew of my previous no contact period, and I felt it best that they knew my final decision. I rang Ross and told him he was lovely and completely understood my decision and did not question it. I sent a very polite but factual letter to my aunt rather than call her. In the letter I focused on Brigittes disorder and the damage that it had caused the family, particularly with regards to healthy communication. I was diplomatic and did not ask her to side with me, as I fully understood her relationship with her sister was a separate matter. I explained that as my younger brother lived with his mum the very dynamic of me going no contact with her would sadly result in me being unable to maintain contact with him.

I mentioned that it also could be possible that mum may retaliate and interfere with my relationship with Ross whom I loved to bits. I signed off stating that I wished the situation could have a happy conclusion for all innocent parties but with the dynamic being as it was that it would be extremely unlikely. I signed off wishing her and Robert all the very best for the future.

A few months passed and during this time I read a great deal about the narcissist mother scapegoat daughter dynamic, and I knew without a shadow of a doubt that I had done the right thing. However, I was a little concerned as I had read many tales of revenge that had been instigated by a narcissist who had been slighted. I predicted the only thing that she could do to spite me was to tell Ross what I had said about his father. I half expected it but hoped with all my heart that it would never happen, but true to form it did.

Song: Way Over Yonder by Carole King

ROOM 8

Spoiler Alert

I am sure that you have guessed from the previous chapter that I have found my real father, and I will reveal all to you nearer the books end. For me to be able to write this in an order which makes sense I have had to introduce this information now because it is relevant to my ever increasingly complex life story.

When I first met dad, he wanted to know all about my childhood. And after a while when I felt comfortable enough in his company, I told him about my stepfather and the two incidents. He was angry and saddened, but I told him that it was in the past, and to let sleeping dogs lie, because it could have been far worse. He understood why I felt the way I did and said that it was important that I dealt with it in a way that kept me in a good and strong headspace. As you will soon discover a real "Long Lost Family" reunion in reality is far different from the TV programme. The initial high is all you see, but many other people are involved in the dynamic. It is an incredibly complex situation, and subsequently some of the people involved are happy and acceptant, and others not so...

I have an older half-brother Bob, who after a period of nine years of not speaking at all to his father, decided to come back onto the scene. Throughout his entire adult life this has been a set theme and was completely unrelated to me finding dad. It was a little awkward, but I was genuinely pleased that they had reconciled, it was also nice to have an older sibling.

Unfortunately, at some point after their reunion dad told Bob about my past and what had happened to me. I suspect it was because his son constantly complains about his childhood, and dad was trying to inject some true perspective into the equation by using me as an example. I was not happy as it was a very personal matter, and one that I most certainly did not want to be made common knowledge.

Bob visited several times after he had offered his olive branch to dad. During one visit he told me that he had an extra SIM card for a contract phone, and he wanted me to have it. I told him that it was nice of him to offer, but I was in a well-paid job, and I was very happy using my pay as you go phone. I wanted to keep the same phone number and also, I am not a person who is constantly glued to my phone or contacting people every five minutes.

To cut a long story short, he wouldn't drop it throughout his stay, and was incredibly overbearing and insistent. He repeatedly said that I was an absolute idiot for not wanting to save money by using a freebie that I could keep. After the fiftieth rejection, I simply agreed just to shut him up and used the card for just over a year, and then suddenly he asked for it back. At the time I thought it a little strange because he told me it was a gift and not on loan. I gave it back to him and got a monthly contract phone with a new number, which I had used for over three years. Everybody knew my number and used it to call me during this time, including Ross. His very last communication directly to me on my phone was after I had a chat with him immediately after my decision to go no contact with mum.

He was in a calm and receptive mood and was very supportive and completely understood my decision. The following day he sent me a text message saying, "Sis please don't be so upset, stay strong you are worth ten of most people, and don't you ever forget it xxx".

I had gone no contact with mum for a few months, and Bob rang me which was very unusual as he normally only spoke to his father directly. He asked if I was ok, and I told him that I was. There was silence for a moment and then he said, "Are you sure you are okay"? and I repeated that I was and was there a reason why he had rung me. He proceeded to say, " I don't want to say, I can't say" to which I told him "That it was not fair to ring someone and worry them, without giving them an explanation".

He then agreed to tell me, and I was horrified at what he began to say. There had been a text to me on his phone from my younger brother saying, "That he had got his father round his throat and was going to kill him, for touching me". And he read other texts in which Ross sounded completely distraught, finishing with a text saying that he hated me.

My mind went into a spin, and I began crying, and I felt sick. I asked when he had received them, to which he responded, "the day before". I wanted to run to Ross and comfort him, but I felt stuck and wretched, I didn't want to confirm what would break his heart. I didn't understand why he was using a very old number, and also, I couldn't comprehend why he had not directly spoken to me to confirm such a terrible discovery. He had also met dad and they got on pretty well and had his number if he urgently needed to speak to me.

At the time of the shocking disclosure, I felt a degree of sadness for my stepfather as he was old and unwell and there was no need to bring the matter up. I knew his time was limited on this earth and he should have been left in peace. I was without doubt that when he passed it would not be forgotten and nor would he be able to lie about it, and that was sufficient for me. It was not for me to judge him, but I knew that ultimately God would.

Bob was diagnosed with ADHD as a child and is in all honesty a Walter Mitty type character, who proudly boasts of possessing "The Warrior Gene". Which is supposedly related to sociopathy and worse. He sadly is a compulsive liar mostly of which are very transparent as they are so outlandish. He also has an extremely unhealthy interest in other people's lives and personal information and possesses the computer skills to utilize data for his own financial ends. This behaviour has led him to be estranged from his entire family apart from his dad. There are issues relating to his behaviour with regards to his "interests and skill sets" that I personally have been on the receiving end of. But it would be unfair to elaborate in further detail as I have not confronted him face to face.

His relationship with dad is very tenuous and I only keep stum as I do not want to rock the boat, which is difficult but necessary, as you will discover later. I do have grave concerns regarding the disclosure, he seemed to play a part in the communication with Ross to what extent I do not know. I simply cannot fathom how the situation seemed to escalate unless Ross was replying to texts that he thought were from me.

I was distraught after the phone call and felt paralysed with regards as to what to do. I could not tip Ross over the edge, so calling him was not an option. I couldn't calm down and I was on the verge of a panic attack, I had not had one for years. It was all too much for me and I was flapping around like a headless chicken and was frantic. I was consumed with thoughts about my poor brother and felt ill.

Suddenly in my right ear the song Turn Turn Turn by The Byrds came very loudly into my head, and I began searching for something that I had a copy of that was related to my dear grandad. Ecclesiastes 3:1-4 which was read at his funeral, he loved it and always told me it was true. I looked immediately for it and found it in my chest of drawers. I sat on my bed and read it repeatedly, until I had settled myself down.

To everything there is a season, and a time to every purpose under the heaven

A time to be born, and a time to die,

A time to plant and a time to pluck up what was planted.

A time to kill, and a time to heal,

A time to break down, and a time to build up

A time to weep, and a time to laugh

A time to mourn, and a time to dance

A time to cast away stones, and a time to gather stones

A time to embrace, and a time to refrain from embracing

A time to get, and a time to lose

A time to keep, and a time to cast away

A time to rend, and a time to sew

A time to keep silence, and a time to speak

A time to love, and a time to hate

A time of war, and a time for peace.

After a week or so I realized that the only course of action available to me was to write a letter to Ross. So, I very carefully worded one explaining that he had been communicating through a third party. I explained about the SIM card, and that he had been using a very old contact number. I went on to infer something had happened which was not great, but could have been far worse. I did not elaborate or give any details about either incident . I told him I had not brought the matter up, and I would never have done so as it had happened such a long time ago. I also said that whoever had let the cat out of the bag was so cruel. And if it was mum, why would she want to hurt him to punish me. I copied a beautiful poem called The Oak Tree, as I felt it applied to both of us, and I wanted him to remain strong. I signed off telling him that I loved him very much, and that he was my only true sibling as we had grown up together. And if he ever needed me, just to reach out his hand and I would always be there for him. And I verified my current phone number so he could ring me if he wanted to talk. The letter was not accusatory or a vilification of his father. it was as fair and gently worded as possible, and extremely difficult to write, I cried buckets whilst doing so.

Ten days later my poor daughter had received a letter from my stepfather, they were not close anymore and had not seen each other for years, due to location and life generally moving on, I didn't actively encourage her having a relationship with him, but she was an adult, and I did not discourage it. She said he had contacted her and had sent a vitriolic letter about me, which she read out. Its contents were a direct attack on me, with no denial of any inappropriate behaviour, it basically said that if he had done such a thing, and I allowed her to see him. It would make me the most disgusting and unfit mother and I should never have had children; it smacked of anger and fear, his true identity shone through in the wording. The fact that I had not elaborated in my letter to Ross what had happened, his direct inference to an indecent assault was a clear admission of culpability, but attack was his only form of defence. Bless her heart Faye sent a response back saying that it was none of her business, and she did not want to get involved. And finally, that it had not been me that had caused this upset and was more than likely my mother.

For several months I hoped that Ross would ring me, but I knew in my heart that he wouldn't. For by doing so it would have placed him in an untenable position. I was without doubt that my stepfather would have churned out the acting performance of his life, vehemently denying any wrongdoing, he was the victim, and I was a crazy liar. I wanted Ross to be happy and if believing his dad enabled him to be able to cope with the situation, it would be best for him and his mental health. No Contact was a walk in the park compared to how bad I felt at losing Ross, he was alive, but I could do nothing. For about a year if I saw someone who looked like him from behind, tears instantly welled up in my eyes. I hoped that time would eventually ease my sadness but knew I would have to be proactive and dig deep to adjust myself to the situation, I was admittedly heartbroken.

My aunt found out about the sorry mess over a year later. And during a nightmare phone call she inferred that I was not being truthful. She could not comprehend that it had not been me who had brought the matter to light. And proceeded to tell me that if in the unlikely event it was true, I was an unfit mother for not telling anyone and allowing my daughter anywhere near him. It was extremely shocking the way she spoke to me. Robert stepped in and took the phone off her, clearly hearing what the conversation was about and the inappropriateness of his wife's words. He said, "Kim please remember that I am your uncle and if you ever need me, I am always here". It was incredibly kind of him; I thanked him and will never forget it. I tried to calm her down too, which was incredible in hindsight. I did not expect anything other than a clinical response from her, but to berate anyone who as a child had been assaulted was not what I considered to be remotely acceptable.

I had always tried to understand her clear intolerance of me and felt that as my birth had caused disruption whilst she was taking her exams, it was somehow justifiable. I felt her resentment towards me was because I played a prominent role in her parent's lives, she was the baby and then I came along. I wondered whether the fact I was clearly suffering abuse was ever raised with her. Perhaps she simply did not know the severity of what I was enduring and how ill it was making me. I wondered whether her childhood around her sister had damaged her, and rather than address the real problem, which was mum whom she may have feared, it was far easier to blame me. I was always trying to make sense of the situation but after the phone call I could no longer do it, she had the problem and not I.

It was an awful time, and I prayed a great deal. The pain and injustice of the situation was difficult for me to get my head round. I knew somehow that I would get through it but I had to do it myself, my faith was my guide, in unison with practical actions. I journalled daily for a couple of months, and all of pain flowed out onto the pages.

I could not speak to those that had hurt me, so I wrote strong letters addressed to them, and then made a point of burning every single page. During this cathartic ceremony I played a beautiful song from the film The Kingdom of Heaven called "Burning the Past" which was extremely appropriate. I listened to music of all genre's Gregorian chants or classical music and songs with motivational lyrics, whatever felt appropriate to my mood I played. I allowed myself to feel anger, the anger that I was never allowed to feel. I set myself a ten-minute time limit to really feel what I had suppressed for many years, and then I moved back to my normal thoughts, I was determined that I would not become embittered.

I read inspirational poems like If by Rudyard Kipling, Desiderata by Max Ehrmann and quotes by philosophers such as Friedrich Nietzsche. They validated my existence in a situation that was completely out of my control. I watched programmes and films with positive and calming narratives. I love watching Robin Williams films as each one he made shows a beautiful genuine quality which made me feel connected.

I looked at a site called Out of the Fog which echoed precisely how I felt. As if I had been in a real pea souper on an ever-spinning roundabout, which I had finally alighted from and was beginning to find my land legs. It had lots of very good tips and information, and I would recommend it to anyone who is going through anything similar.

Although I felt mentally exhausted and sometimes, I truly felt like lying in bed and sleeping the days away. I forced myself to do what I normally did when life was calm and relatively trouble free.

I went outside for walks because nature is a wonderful healer, and the beauty of this earth is second to none. I looked beyond myself as a human being, and at bigger spaces such as the sea, the clouds and the sky. I looked properly at the people around me and noticed all the sad, lonely and very poor. Because there has to be a gauge based on reality to assess yourself or others accurately by. If you reflect truthfully on what has happened to you from a logical standpoint you will not become self-absorbed and you will heal, it truly is within us all. There will always be someone "more hurt" than you out there in the world. And that alone is enough motivation to move past and heal any damage that is within us, for they may not be able to. There is so much "out there" that will comfort you, but to do so you must look beyond yourself and really look, and you will be surprised at what you will discover.

Songs: Breath of Life by Erasure

Eleanor Rigby by The Beatles

Poem: The Oak Tree by Johnny Ray Ryder

THE WARDROBE 9

A Little About My Suit

And so that is my back story, no great shakes in the grander scheme of things but I would be lying if I said that it hadn't affected me because it did. And although I have never actively planned suicide, there have been a few times in my life when I have wished for an easy cop out. I wished that God would take me in my sleep and away from a world that was so cruel and unfair. But when I awoke the following day, although I was extremely tired. I was always relieved to see another day.

My survival instinct is very strong but some dear sweet souls are completely overtaken by life's events. If I was able to sit next to them on the bridge, or when they reach for the pills, a rope or a razor blade. I would do all that I could to give them hope and I would give them the biggest of bear hugs. Two of the most moving adverts on the telly are the SOS Silence of Suicide adverts which are beyond poignant. I too have smiled many times through heartache, and it is true that those who commit suicide are the people who you would least expect to follow it through. Sometimes we simply cannot carry our own water because the load is too much to bare. Hats off to all help lines like this and The Samaritans. If you feel really down, please turn to them, or speak to a friend and open up.

However past events will never change the style of my earthly suit. Which is admittedly a bit baggier with age, but the cut and pattern still suits me. My favourite outfit when I was in my early twenties was a man's suit that I brought from my local charity shop. It was grey flannel with thin white pinstripes and was also a little baggy. But this was intentional so I could wear a very wide black belt to accentuate my once very thin waist. Worn with red stiletto's it was my favourite clubbing outfit and I felt like the mutt's nuts when I wore it.

People often used to say that I looked like Princess Diana when I was younger, which was a massive compliment. I was more tomboyish though and didn't like wearing skirts. However, if I had a job interview my to the knee Prince of Wales check mini was dragged from the back of the wardrobe for a "gissa job airing", worn with a double-breasted black blazer with gold buttons, black turtleneck jumper and black suede pumps it never failed.

I thought Princess Diana was extremely genuine, a little troubled maybe, but she came from a place of truth and was incredibly empathetic. Strangely enough my aunt once did an ancestry search and discovered that grans family went directly back to Barbara of Castlemaine (7 x great grandmother). Who was a bit of an iffy mistress of Charles the Second, and a couple of her five children were purportedly his. Apparently, Princess Diana's ancestors went directly back to Charles the

Second, down the legitimate route unlike us! I was terribly sad when she died, she was such a kind genuine individual, and one that most of us could relate to.

I Love

God, Potatoes, Old School Trance, Running in the Sea Without Rolling up my Jeans, Wotsits, Golden Syrup, Waterfalls, Wood Pigeons, Pink and White Roses, William Morris, Riverdance and Musical Boxes

Dislikes

Drill Rap, Feet, Marrows, Hypocrisy, Flies, Luxury Values, Bad Manners, Tuneless Whistling, The Singing Ringing Tree, Pork Chops, Arrogance, Heavy Metal, Snakes, Turkish Delight, Pork Belly, Fake Smiles, People who do not say thank you when they are given their newly restored item on The Repair Shop.

Just A Very Few of The Many Suits that I would love to have a chat with

Jesus (INFJ), King David, George Harrison,(INFJ), Martin Luther King Jnr (INFJ), Billy Connelly, Paul O'Grady, Avicii, Gary Barlow, Keanu Reeves, Oskar Schindler, Sandy Toksvig, John Wayne, Prince ,Chad Ripperger, Bob Mortimer, Robin Williams, Devin Gibson, Burt Lancaster, The Queen, Douglas

Murray, Tiesto, Freddie Mercury, Alan Carr, Anne Frank, Carole Malone, Ben Fogle, David Suchet, Paddy Mayne, John Le Mesurier, Colin Brazier, Rik Mayall, Kap Chatfield, Jim Carey, Amanda Holden, Rob Rinder, JK Rowlings (INFJ), Paul Whitehouse, Noel Fitzpatrick, Derek Prince, Iain Duncan Smith, Dobbie, Mel Gibson, Ant & Dec, Nana Akua, Jennifer Saunders, Lord Craig Makinlay, Rylan Clark, Kate Middleton, Yonan Netanyahu, Jordan Peterson, Andrew Doyle, Derren Brown (INFJ), Simon Khorolskiy, Vangelis, Moya Brennan, Akaine Kramarick, George Orwell, Jim Caviezel, Morgan Freeman (INFJ) and David Niven.

A Few of My Favourite Films

The Passion of The Christ, Awakenings, Good Will Hunting, The Shootist, Operation Daybreak, True Grit, Dances with Wolves, Rebecca, Shadowlands, The Shawshank Redemption, ET, Tootsie, Mrs Doubtfire, Braveheart, Mrs Brown, City of Angels, The Last Samurai, Wuthering Heights (1939 version) A Christmas Carol (Alistair Sims version) and Drop Dead Fred.

Programmes That I Love

Mortimer & Whitehouse Go Fishing, The Repair Shop, Ben Fogle New Lives in The Wild, Great Pottery Throwdown, Alan & Amanda's Italian Job, The Good Place, Touched by An Angel, The Doghouse, Poldark, Interior Design Masters,

Britain's Got Talent, Great British Sewing Bee, and SAS Who Dares Wins.

Past Crushes

Captain Kirk, David Soul, David Essex, Jason Connery, Christopher Cazenove and Bryan Adams.

Favourite Smells

Candy Floss, Lemons and Witch Hazel.

Favourite Authors... In No Particular Order

Elly Griffiths, Mark Manson, Daphne Du Maurier, Adele Parks, Lisa Jewell, Clare McGowan and Judy Finnegan.

Favourite Albums (If I could only pick two, one would be pushing it)

The Very Best of Fleetwood Mac, 1492 by Vangelis

Favourite Poet

Becky Hemsley

Tours Compilation Album # An Excuse for Me to Add Some More Songs!

Baby When Your Gone by Bryan Adams and Mel C, When Doves Cry by Prince, Don't Stop Believing by Journey, Kiss From a Rose by Seal, Wichita Lineman by Glen Campbell, Let's Dance by David Bowie, The Zepher Song by The Red Hot Chilli Peppers, Rockstar by Nickelback, Hey Soul Sister by Train, Don't Speak by No Doubt, If You Could Read My Mind by Gordon Lightfoot, The Logical Song by Supertramp, Little Bird by Annie Lennox, Africa by Toto, Here With Me by Dido, I Will Find You and Harrys Game by Clannad, Here Comes The Sun and Hey Jude by The Beatles, What's Up by 4 Non Blondes, Fix You by Coldplay, Baker Street by Gerry Rafferty, The Boy That Wouldn't Hoe Corn Dan Tyminski, Whenever Wherever by Shakira, Your Song by Elton John, Everybody Wants to Rule The World by Tears for Fears, Sound of Silence by Simon and Garfunkel, Don't You Worry Child Swedish House Mafia, Running Up the Hill by Kate Bush, Losing My Religion and Everybody Hurts by REM, Call Me Al by Paul Simon, Sledgehammer by Peter Gabriel, Don't Stop Me Now by Queen, I'm Not In Love by 10cc, When the Going Gets Tough by Billy Ocean, Wayfaring Stranger by

Adam Chance and The Hound and The Fox, Exodus by Andy Williams, Children by Robert Miles.

And finally, my latest favourite is Levels by Avicii I can totally relate to the video as like so many of us I have been silenced by others. But I will always continue to speak out, regardless of how many times the stun silencer gun is used on me. And just between us I often dance round the house and do some crazy moves just like the guy in the video, and I care not a jot what anyone thinks of me.

So, this is obligatory please play the song, but you must strut your crazy stuff, as best as you are able and never let others silence you, when your words are for the good.

God Bless you Avicii a soul who was very intune spiritually and with life and its whole dynamic. He knew the score and put brilliant videos "out there" for us all to see. Thank you for sharing your message with us through your "Calling" There are many of us out there just like you, and we all send you, our love. xxx

ROOM 10

Little George & His Pal Jiminy Cricket

I have discovered on my literary journey that many agents specifically request submissions from minority groups who fall under the classification of being underrepresented, and some of whom undoubtedly are. However, this very specific request has relegated other groups such as the working class who fall under precisely the same classification very firmly to the back of the queue. I was truly shocked to discover one agency who professed to be the literary champion go to for all those in "minority groups" had a client/author list the majority of whom were of colour and were in very high-profile careers relating to literature and journalism in organizations such as the BBC. Their careers were further endorsed and advanced by an agency which receives public funding. I would say that is somewhat unfair although they may fall under a minority heading, it is in name only as their voices are already being heard, they are not in the least bit "underrepresented". They may well have written excellent books and are very decent individuals it is not about talent or personality, it is about the current dynamic throughout most of the literary world, which seems to have become a box ticking exercise.

Barriers which are placed before us that advocate and promote inequality need to be spoken about, it is not about my success or lack of it is simply unfair. I should not be placed before another human being for any reason and nor should another be placed before me. We should be given equal opportunities and earn any advantages or benefits solely on merit nothing more nothing less.

I find many things offensive as an INFJ and an HSP, particularly depictions of violence and cruelty or very overt sexual scenes, described in books or on the telly. My personal character traits are not another person's issue but my own, there are millions of sensitive souls out there. What should we all do? Tell the powers that be, that we feel sick and distressed at the amount of unhealthy material being shown, aired or published, which incites copycat behaviour, and therefore should be censored, cancelled and banned? No, we make a conscious decision to not watch, listen or read anything that may offend or upset us. The point I am making here is relevant, as a person that belongs to two groups of people who have been proven psychologically to think and react in a very particular way. How is it that an actual and real personal sensitivity does not even register? I shall tell you why, it is because there is no benefit to include us. Protecting our sensibilities and feelings will not earn elitest groups any virtue signalling brownie points from within in their inner circle. I like many others have experienced sadness and I am officially sensitive, so by rights I should fit the criteria necessary to be a sensitivity reader, however the very thought of being one is abhorrent to me.

A gradual introduction of things like this may seem innocuous and harmless but you must look at the bigger picture. As by not questioning the actual relevance or validity of what at face value seems to be a small and isolated idea, more similar are permitted. And before you know it a whole new set of ideas are accepted as the collective norm; new ideologies can very quickly become a way of life and be detrimental. We are at a point in history when we are gradually losing our personal right to an opinion. And anyone who engages in censorship that is not truly necessary, will have played a role in contributing to an Orwellian dystopian future and be it on their own heads.

Graphic descriptions of serial killers modus operandi and methods of killing or fictional horror stories depicting horrific subject matter, are fine and dandy. However, if a person inadvertently uses one of the latest cancelled words, or even worse dare to question a stance or have an opinion of their own all hell is let loose. There clearly are beyond incredible double standards with regards to what information is deemed acceptable. There is nothing within this book that could be interpreted as remotely offensive, much has already been said by others both verbally, and within newspapers and books which have been written by authors and journalists who I have a tremendous amount of respect for.

I am terribly saddened that my discovery has led me to the conclusion that without a shadow of a doubt thousands of relatable non-fiction books are not even considered. A market which will never be endorsed or promoted by those within an elitist bubble. One that is merely an echo chamber for those within it and not an actual true representation of the wider population. A market well and truly missed by the industry, presumably they think that people like me do not purchase books or read them. However, this could not be further from the truth, I read many books of all genres.

The loss of thousands of stories drowned in a mire of group think, which seems to be based on elitism or abject terror, which stymies those within into a state of complacency and inertia. Ultimately publishing houses have the last word and I can understand that some literary agents probably do feel like their hands are tied and cannot afford to get a publisher offside. Of course, if a book has subject matter that incites hatred it should not be published, however when it has the reverse intent it should be given a chance if it merits one.

I do not believe for one moment that all literary agents have elitest extreme left-wing views and on the QT, I am sure that many have precisely the same views and values as the rest of us. However, I suspect that many have been bound by fear-based constraints and have unspoken criteria imposed on them which they must adhere to. It is incredibly difficult to put your head above the parapet in situations such as these and I totally get it. However, following the herd when they are indisputably correct is fine, but when there is an alternative viewpoint which can break down barriers that impede and affect us all, surely it is better to be a maverick and stand alone, as often others will follow your lead.

So, there you have it I have managed in "plain sight" to sneak in a wee rant about the unfairness of the literary industry and the part it has played in discouraging healthy debate. I would recommend that you research the subject as it is terribly important. Books record history and the thoughts of all those that have lived during a period, we cannot make informed decisions and improve the future, when we do not have a true representation of the past. And without exception all voices should be heard, unless they are inciting hatred.

It buoyed me to discover that the author Chimamanda Ngozi Adichie who has written several novels including Purple Hibiscus, has recently been discussing the literary world; with regards to freedom of expression and denied truths. She is also incredibly worried about creeping authoritarianism, fake news and democracy currently failing. As well as being greatly concerned about authors feeling it necessary to self-censor.

She has echoed far more eloquently than I am able the following....

"Books shape our understanding of the world. We speak of Dickensian London. We look to great African writers like Aidoo and Ngugi to understand the continent and we read Balzac for the subtitles of post-Napoleonic France. Literature deeply matters and I believe it is in peril because of self-censure. If nothing changes the next generation will read us and wonder, how did they manage to stop being human. How were they so lacking in contradiction and complexity. How did they banish all their shadows?"

In her recent Reith Lecture, she made a passionate call to arms and argued that our culture of self-censorship, policing each other's language, cordoning off whole subjects as unsayable is "almost the death knell of literary and other cultural production. If we cannot tell the truth to one another literature is finished."

I agree whole heartedly, the proverbial non-fiction literary funeral has been planned with meticulous detail, and the final nail will soon be driven into the very generic plain coffin.

Song: Road to Nowhere by Talking Heads

ROOM 11

Growing Old, Ego's & Faith

This is going to be a room in which I shall ramble on about subjects which are very important to me. I may find it necessary to break my Trevor and Simon pledge and partake in a spot of non-duvet padding, which may help The Manor achieve its Trivago 77777-star rating.

When reading a book, I can normally tell when an author is trying to reach a set word count or a particular goal. Repetition becomes the order of the day, descriptions become far lengthier and new characters briefly appear for a hundred words or so, and then are not mentioned again. I imagine the author sitting at their computer yawning, desperate to hit the sack, and thinking I have got to eek this out for another three chapters. The writing style changes and becomes lazier and instead of reading enthusiastically, I begin to skim the pages for anything that is relevant to the books ending. But as I am fully invested in the plot, I plough through like my newly adopted literary hero until the bitter end.... And then I am gutted when I have finished the book and wish I hadn't gone into speed reading mode.

I can't add any extra characters as this is a non-fiction book. Well perhaps I could, but it would be a fantasy involving

Robert Redford re-enacting his role as the Sundance Kid with me playing his companion Etta Place. Not now I hasten to add but when we were both in our prime.

Today I am absolutely knackered as I have been up since 3.30 am. I am post-menopausal, and my body has decided in its infinite wisdom, that I only need four or five hours sleep a night maximum, and I actually feel a little punch drunk today. I normally go back to sleep after a couple of hours but this morning I didn't because I had a dentist appointment. Which I wouldn't normally be worried about; but the appointment today was regarding a wisdom tooth that needs to be extracted. And as the procedure would normally be done under a general anaesthetic that was enough to send my mind into overdrive. Pathetic I know but to me being put under equates to death.

Prior to my early morning mental chat with myself that was about anything and everything that had little to no relevance, I had a lovely dream. What the hell stage of sleep I had entered at this stage I dread to think. Science would dictate REM, but it certainly was not refreshing, and I woke up feeling like I had been run over by the RWE Bagger 288.

In my REM state I was frog marched over to one of a line of dentist chairs all of which had patients laying on them, with carrier bags over their heads. All were lifeless of course, and unsurprisingly I knew at that point what fate lay in store for me. A woman was standing beside the chair with a bag and some gaffer tape in hand, in readiness to make the world a far better place. Naturally only in her sick and delusional mind, but I knew that there was no point in trying to convince her otherwise.

She was wearing a decidedly dodgy nylon baby pink jumper and a very unattractive floral polyester A line skirt. A similar outfit to one that was donned by a previous work manager who micro-managed the very life out of me. It will come as no surprise that we didn't work together very long. Facially she looked like the prisoner Bea Smith from Prisoner Cell Block H.

All her murder victims had been duped into believing it was a routine dental procedure, but I was having none of it. I turned on my heels and ran out of the practice, and straight into the comfort of my own bed. And then after what seemed like no more than thirty minutes, a new day had dawned.

After a cup of biscuit tea, I trudged up to the cold storage unit in the house, which is multi-functional, and can also be used as a cryogenic chamber or when desperate the bathroom. After defrosting my nemesis, the magnification X 5 mirror. I then set about preparing my face for the day, which believe me is not an easy task. Trying to apply mascara to your remaining treasured lashes in a way that does not enter "Baby Jane" territory is no mean feat. I have tried every mascara going, I find one that almost works and then I decide that there possibly is one out there that will achieve my desired look. I may as well be searching for the Holy Grail, which I would be far more likely to find. Back in the day I swear there was only three brands of mascara Outdoor Girl, Rimmel and Max Factor. Three colour options black, brown and electric blue. Blue was only ever worn if you wanted to try out a new look down the local nightclub, or you were having a serious personal crisis. Now there are so many ranges and most of them are formulated to make your eyelashes look super long, or volume enhanced. I don't mind trying to extend mine but volume enhancing X 24.75 is to be avoided at all costs.

The less is more look is by far the safest bet, because it enables you to remain under the radar in public and looking of sound mind. But the annoying thing is to achieve the invisible woman look, you have to apply more slap than you have ever applied in your entire life, and it takes a very steady hand. And after four- or five-hours sleep, I get sloppy and invariably miss my eye lashes. I reach for my Poundland wipes and start again. For a spot of light relief, I secretly perform the instant two finger facelift, hold it for a few seconds, pull my hands away and watch my face immediately drop back into its slack position. As I am starting to resemble a ventriloquist's dummy, I decide to fully commit and say "Gottle of Geer". After twenty minutes of applying and reapplying all manner of preparations, I feel like giving up the ghost and retiring to my bed to have a well-deserved nanna nap. Today was no different and with no

Barbara Daly on hand, it took me ages to prepare my face for the day.

Bea her bag and gaffer tape were awaiting my arrival...

And when I attended my appointment, I saw one of the nicest dentists and dental nurses I had ever met. And as luck would have it the dentist decided that because one of my roots is curled and very close to a nerve, an extraction was too risky. Oh, happy days, no anaesthetic for me and I remained on a natural high for the rest of the day, I had been worrying over nothing. Little wins have always made me happy, and I am so glad that they do. An old friend used to say when anything good had happened to her " I am as chuffed as a carrot" which is an absolute classic, so much so that it should go global, please pass the orange love on.

It's 7.30 pm on a January evening and I am freezing my arse off in my semi. Like most of you I am reluctant to put my heating on and swell the coffers of my energy company. Which I better not name as they may send the heavies round and install a smart meter, and I would not be a happy bunny. I have the most awful lilac fleece hoodie on that I brought from Primani and an electric throw over my legs. Probably not the wisest thing placing the laptop on top of it, but needs must, if it was to overheat, I am so blinking cold I would barely notice.

A time of real and genuine hardship for many that highlights true poverty more than ever. It's a crying shame that those who constantly promote a humanitarian stance do not have a true gauge as to what is true and real suffering. The word humanitarian is often used by people to describe themselves, which makes a mockery of the word and denotes the need to inflate personal ego in the form of self-promotion with the aim to receive accolades and awards. True acts of kindness are performed by those who do not wish to self-promote, for it would invalidate their true altruistic intentions. The dictionary definition of the word is "having concern for or helping to improve the welfare and happiness of people or relating to ethical or theological humanitarianism". I would like to think the majority of the world cares about their fellow man, kindness is not a marketable or exclusive commodity and should never be used as such. I can't think for a minute who I could possibly be referring too!

This I hasten to add applies only to one person out of the duo. Who without question is one of the "haughty eyes" brigade. It saddens me tremendously that Harry has been ensnared by her and as sure as eggs are eggs, he will soon be superfluous to requirements. For he is becoming of little to no use to her or her be good and kind and very rich and influential buddies.

When he comes back to the Country, he will be confused and very damaged by the whole experience, and I hope that he is cut some slack by the British public. And also, if we welcome him back with open arms, it sends a very clear message to the source of all this upset. Princess Diana was extremely astute and I am sure she would have seen right through Meghan if she had ever met her. And Harry would not have been in the sad situation he is now. He would be having a laugh with William and Kate, and would have found a wife that had not actively sought him out. But one who would have loved him for the man he is inside and not his title.

Although at times it, may seem that the flashy designer cashmere suits hold all of the cards, clothes do not maketh the man. And on close inspection you will see their suits are infact fake and made from the cheapest of materials. Whilst those who appear to be wearing budget polyester suits are enrobed in the most luxurious velvet, which will always cushion and nurture their soul.

If you met me, I would like to think you would find me kind, very down to earth, with a very dry sense of humour but extremely logical and practical. I do not normally discuss my faith with anyone. But as it is my contractual obligation to do so instead of "Breaking Bad" I am "Breaking Some Good". If you are expecting me to start spouting religious terms and becoming all preachy on you, rest assured that this is not going to happen. Because I wouldn't know how to or were to start and it really isn't me.

As you know I have believed from the earliest of ages and I have always prayed. However, I only read small passages from the bible, bite sized portions that made sense but were insufficient to understand the book as a whole. I did try several times to read it in one go but I found it a little heavy going. Patience is something that I struggle with and is a work in progress. When I eventually took the plunge and read it in full it is a wonderful book and the perfect moral compass. And of course, I wish I had read it sooner but better late than never and its message was what I expected. A few things did surprise me: the first being the incredible amount of detail given with regards to dimensions, weights, numbers, materials and names. And what I took from that is... if you are doubting what we are saying then don't, we are being beyond precise here, to confirm the accuracy of all of the experiences and events throughout. Also, the Godly supernatural element surprised me there were far more events than I expected as did the symmetrical themes. I would say to anyone who wants to read the bible but is a little daunted by the prospect. Listen on YouTube to the wonderful David Suchet who has narrated it in its entirety. He brings it to life and when I want to refer to a particular section of it David is my go-to.

As I am introverted my faith has been in all honesty my own little security blanket. Because I know that there is a God, I felt no real need to discuss it with anyone. Partly because if I kept it secret, then people would not know that I had something to draw on when they were being cruel or unkind. I expect that sounds a little crazy, but it was almost like a shield of protection that others could not see, and if I shared it with others, it may lose its potency, which of course is not the case.

Faith and religion are only as complicated as you want to make it. Although I may seem a little complex, I am not, and this is also reflected in my faith. It may or may not surprise you but I do not attend a church. I prefer going into a church when it is empty so I can pray and quietly reflect. My personal church in which I feel at peace is outside in nature. I love walking on the beach and if I had to chose one location to pray the beach would be it. If I want to listen to anyone preach I listen to Derek Prince on YouTube who is sadly no longer with us.

If I could insert a heart bullet point alongside each of the things that I believe I would. But as this version of Microsoft word does nothing beyond letting me type, I will settle for a diamond. As in "Shine Bright Like a Diamond", and no surprises there isn't one. So as a basic circle is the only option available it will represent the " Circle of Life". I loved the theatre version of the Lion King, and when the Broadway cast took over a train on the New York subway and sung the song, it was such a wonderful feel-good moment, which without fail makes me cry, as does the finale of Riverdance.

Kim's Circles of Life

- I believe that there is One God and Jesus is his Son.

- I say the Lord's Prayer and Psalm 23 each day and a personal non-scripted prayer of gratitude for all the things I am blessed to have. This is for the simple things that many people take for granted. Food in my stomach, the roof over my head, my life, my family, my friends, my health, and above all God. Who regardless of our many earthly sins forgives those who truly are sorry for the hurt that they have caused others. I don't want to burst your bubble if you consider yourself to be perfect, but none of us are. We muck up sometimes deliberately and sometimes inadvertently. And we also may have unknowingly sinned and thought something we did was acceptable when it was not. I pray for the world and for the people in it, and for Gods light to shine in the darkest of places. I say whatever I feel as God is my Father my confident and my rock and he always listens. Whether you pray within a group or on your own like me, it is better to pray than not to pray at all.

- Any terrorist group who professes to fight in God's name and who kill any of Gods children have absolutely nothing to do with God. And are infact batting for the other spiritual side.

- I believe that the main cause of the world's problems is due to man believing only in himself and his desire to constantly fuel his ego. Subsequently there is no off button for many people; fame, greed, power, control, violence and supremacy they will stop at nothing to achieve their goals. And with no apparent ramifications for their actions and no moral compass to follow they see no need to stop. We are currently in a state of spiritual warfare, on many different levels. And Leaders of Countries who discourage religion through intimidation, know the power of faith, and are very scared of the power and inner confidence and strength that it gives people.

- God has gone beyond being disappointed and is absolutely mortified at what the world has become. Whether you believe me or not he is letting us know just how annoyed he is.

- I believe that sadly there is currently a degree of corruption within the ranks of all denominations.

- There are millions of good souls from all religions who genuinely have faith and wish to spread good, however sadly some are hypocritical, self-promoting, greedy and truthfully some bat for the other side, as in the opposite of good intent. People such as the nuns particularly in Ireland that stole babies from vulnerable mothers for financial gain, or those from all denominations that abuse children under the guise of representing God. These people have precisely zip all to do with true faith and their actions have actually turned people away from a beautiful and kind belief system which is such a crying shame.

The problem is there are many people like this in the world who use a platform for their own ends. I was recently discussing this subject with my best friend and she told me a story about the actor Jim Carey. A few years in America there was a trend of feeding the homeless, filming it and then putting it online for the world to see your good deeds. Children were introduced into the dynamic and they would hand over some food and ask when the poor soul had last eaten. It went on for months and finally Jim publicly spoke up and told all who were filming a "good deed" to stop it as it was invalidating real acts of kindness that do not need to be witnessed by an audience.

My faith is very strong and unshakeable and a prayer spoken truly from the heart even in your own home is always listened to. And if you attend church for the wrong reasons and only do so to make a public display of your supposed goodness and righteousness, you are on an absolute hiding to nothing. God will not listen regardless of your sacred location. He is only interested in what is in your heart and if you have good intentions, he is all ears wherever you choose to pray.

For at least thirty years I have become increasingly aware that many people are gradually becoming spiritually "switched off". Whether through choice or they have been influenced by external forces which are media led. I have always referred to them as "the eyes wide shut brigade". It is high time to try and awaken them from their slumber.

Before we go on to the next two rooms, please feel free to leave any unnecessary excess baggage you may have accidently brought with you. We have spent at least a couple of hours together and I have rabbited on whilst you have patiently listened, and I thank you for remaining with me. I have divulged more to you than anyone else in the world, no one knows me as well as you. You know my past which has been like many others unremarkable in many aspects, but unique to me. You know to a degree what makes me tick, and like most people I am multi-dimensional.

Our views about personal matters that have been based on our lived experiences are only a very small part of our identity. Many of us think beyond ourselves and our own thoughts and think about the world and how we can improve it. Solutions to global problems are never found by using opinions which are based solely on emotions. They can only be addressed by using honesty, common sense, logic and facts, and then and only then will things ever begin to improve.

Although my core identity is grounded in my faith which separates Christians from the worldly and earthly dynamic. Because we have a long-term vision which has nothing to do with our physical bodies. The bottom line is we all have to live here for however long we have been allotted and I like millions of others want the world to be fair and peaceful, with no group trying to oppress another in any way shape or form.

Christianity does not equate to foolishness, all the prominent and good souls in the bible were incredibly discerning, they all had to be incredibly astute and very brave when faced with evil doers, whether as a group or facing an individual. They often lost battles but they won many and always won the war. David won his battle against Goliath by trusting in God and slinging a single stone at Goliath's forehead. Throughout the bible there are stories of the bad guys getting above their station, being greedy and out of control and worshipping Baal.

They weren't just left to their own devices and forgiven all of the wicked and evil acts that they did to others. Of course, we must forgive others if we can, but some evil acts are truly unforgivable. It is far better to be discerning and avoid conflict but to do this in all situations whether personal, or global, setting boundaries and using common sense is vital. There is no place at the moment for naivety and spouting off opinions, that are based solely on emotions which are not remotely formed on experience, data, facts and figures.

There are many faiths around the world who simply want to live in peace and they do not desire war. Just as I believe in God the Father, His Son Jesus and the Holy Spirit. Culture and location have dictated that others have different faiths and belief systems. My faith and religion does not have to be someone else's, harmony and unity should be all human beings' goal, but sadly currently this is not the case.

I am passionate about the world, and I am opinionated because our world matters. I often shout at the telly when I see or hear something that is unfair. And I will gently give my opinion if someone states something is a fact when it is not. My opinion has been formed from experience, statistics, facts and data. And I do not argue or push my point onto anyone, and so the following chapter is my opinion on the current state of the world, and no one else's but mine. I am an autonomous individual and I do not follow the herd, I never have and I never will. Even if some of the people in my life do, I still love them and respect their opinions, and the feeling is mutual.

I appreciate that the "Heal the world make it a better place" may sound all very Mary Poppins and a little nausea inducing. But my personality is far more Billy Connolly. I love sweary observational humour, and the man is an absolute genius. I embrace my silver hair which is neither one thing nor the other, half curly, half straight and when I don't do anything with it. it is my homage to Billy. And often when I wake up in the morning and I catch a glimpse of myself in the mirror I utter to myself " Great I have got a face, like a shit house rat" not that I have seen one and nor would I want to.

And so, I am admittedly not a stereotypical Christian; I have a couple of tattoos and I drink twice a week. I am a real person with flaws. I have made shed loads of mistakes in my life and I have never pretended otherwise. But Mary also has a place within me, and comes to the fore when she is needed to be on duty. Recently she brought a bunch of flowers for an elderly lady who was sitting near her in the local supermarket's cafe, just because she wanted to bring a smile to the lady's face, and to make her feel still part of the world. So, when she does a shift, she will always introduce some pure but very unrefined sugar to help the truth go down, and she will do so in her usual and most delightful way.

And now a quick recommendation for a laugh...

The Dwarf on the Bus... The Wonderful Billy Connolly :)

Songs: Days Of Pearly Spencer by David McWilliams

Piano Inclinato (From Rocco Schiavonne) by Corrado Carosio

THE TOILET 12

Let's Try & Stop Us Going Right Down the Proverbial

I love watching an Italian tv series called Rocco Schiavone, which is about a world-weary but very kind maverick detective. He has an annoyance scale, which ranges between one to ten, one being the least annoying. And a frustrating murder case or dealing with incompetent or rude people will usually get a score of 9. And he never fails to let everyone in the vicinity know when he is reaching that point. Many things are currently pressing my buttons, so I am going to implement The Rocco Scale for this chapter, and it will get a score of 10 from me so run for the hills!

There needs to be a lot more sense in this world and MIDDLE GROUND I don't normally do shouty capitals, but the world is currently crazy, and needs must.

I make a character assessment of a person by the way they conduct themselves around me, not as a class, a colour, a disability or a gender. If they are kind and care about their fellow man as best as they are able, then we can coexist very happily. And I expect to be judged by precisely the same set of standards, it is two-way traffic and there are no excuses for bad behaviour. Whether in the majority or the minority neither group should play the victim card to excuse poor and unacceptable behaviour, there should be no get out of jail free cards issued to any of us.

We must all try and get along the best way we can and accept one and other, if our hearts are good, unity should be are only goal. There are some truly terrible and evil people in the world orchestrating more than enough trouble and heinous acts. Global in fighting is playing directly into whatever wishes our downfall, be it a person a Country or some sort of decidedly dodgy negative energy, one or all three we cannot allow this to continue. There have been terrible injustices throughout history: slavery and murders of many groups of people, of all ethnicities, colour and faiths. Unless the world achieves a state of utopia these atrocities will always happen.

The African slave trade was horrific and one of the first serious programmes I watched was Roots. I cried at a scene when Kunta Kinte was being flogged it almost made me vomit. The same revulsion is instilled in me when I see footage of the Holocaust, how in God's name could anyone do that to another person? Both are evil acts different reasons, different coloured "suits" precisely the same outcome. Situations that should never be repeated, but it is in China right now to people that have a suit that would be classed as an in-between shade of the ones I have listed above. All the information is there if you look on the internet and research the Country in question it is not hidden in the least, it is a matter whether you choose to be aware of it or not. The Uighurs are suffering terribly as are the Falun Gong Monks and the Chinese citizens who are not sticking precisely to the parties' medieval rules. I have looked at some beyond terrible images and footage and it is akin to the holocaust and God forbid it may even be a little worse. It affected me greatly and I had to stop researching as I would have made myself ill. I pray for the poor people who are stuck in a beautiful Country with no rights or opinions permitted. Infighting is pathetic now, rehashing the same old grievances and not addressing real and current world problems such as mass genocide is absolutely shameful.

Marxism, fascism, communism, and totalitarianism are precisely all the same in the scheme of things, all based on power skewed extremist narratives designed to ultimately control the world. Some are subtle and hide under the guise of fairness and equality, but the true root of these groups can always be sourced straight back to the power hungry, greedy or truthfully the outright evil. Those that follow are either directly complicit, coerced by threats such as blackmail or simply in desperate need of a group to identify with. The young are also targeted, some of whom are not life experienced enough to assess the facts and would believe that a manifesto directly aimed at them as being the truth.

Which is not their fault, but the bad will always seek out the good and utilise any opportunity if it is presented, and poxy social media is their perfect means of doing so. I firmly reject and rebuke every one of these awful, polarized groups that use every means possible: the threat of ostracism, fear, intimidation and ultimately death.

And the more of us that stand strong and united in any way that we can to neutralise these oppressive and corrupt groups the better. It could be the smallest of actions but magnify it by millions of like-minded people doing precisely the same, the result could be a cohesive and peaceful world. Whatever earthly suit a person has it shouldn't matter because essentially, we are all the same. If you are rich beyond your wildest dreams but have remained truly humble your soul and true essence will never change. Because you understand that you are just a suit who happens to have more material items than others. But when your wealth or your public status are used to influence others or to try to control narratives that are not yours to control then your soul will reduce in size. Although there will be no ramifications in this materialistic and ego driven world, there will be in the next.

I find people who control others by professing to be nice far worse than those who overtly do so. At least when you see a person is armed you are fully prepared, but I find the creepy do gooders insidious. Smiling and bunging money at causes close to their heart which in many cases is not a true one. There are many groups out there who do this, and take back handers and use money to control a dynamic or to push a particular point, rules and the law of the land do not apply to them.

One such group that we are all aware of is the Freemasons. Most of us will know someone who is part of this supposedly quirky and harmless group. And in all honesty, I don't care what they believe and do. But when members of this group infiltrate the Church and preach to others, or give Communion then it is offensive and blasphemous. Of course they should be permitted to sit in the congregation and repent like we all must do. But they should not be permitted to stand before people who believe in the one and only God. Whilst they descend down the 33 degree slippery slope, and wish to see a pagan God called Jahbulon. Which is a hybrid unholy trinity comprising of three ancient Middle Eastern Gods, Jah, God of the Jews, Baal, God of the Phoenicians, and Osiris an Egyptian God. The God Baal is in the bible and is a false prophet which represents the devil, and Osiris ruled over the abode of the dead. Many authors have written about this subject, which is how I found this information. I recently watched a very informative post on YouTube by The Living World Church called "Freemasonry EXPOSED Watch this before it is banned". Hopefully it won't be, and you take a look at it. The pastor explains the whole dynamic and why it is so dangerous for those who join, their families and above all our society.

There are millions of Freemasons doing what they do, and as I said each to their own. But Jesus did not tolerate such practices in houses of God, and he drove out all those who were buying and selling in a temple. He overturned the tables of the money changers and the seats of those who were selling doves. And said to them, "It is written, my house shall be called a house of prayer, but you are making it a robber's den". Churches should be clean and I pray that all clergy who represent God, are brave enough to have a thorough spiritual spring clean, if one is necessary.

Just one of many elitist groups, who hide in plain sight and will use projection, to deflect the attention away from themselves and directly onto others, to silence them so they can maintain absolute control. People are told that they are crazy if they point the finger at them, a nutty conspiracy theorist, and they will all back each other up when push comes to shove.

Large companies, governments and established institutions will always have people from these groups within the mix, and until there is the very final spiritual battle this will continue. Many have to swear allegiance to the group and betrayal in any way would result in punishment of some sort, either financial ruin or death. Without doubt some join up to progress further in this material world and are fed a completely false narrative. And sadly, before they know it, they are rendered inert and are in far too deep to ever be able to leave, and I feel sorry for those who are currently in this position.

Recently I found a couple of short clips that the BBC had put on line discussing the "myths" surrounding The Illuminati and, in all honesty, it made no sense. They shot the very idea down in flames by discrediting a couple of authors who had written books about it in the 1960's. And one of them had apparently said that Paul McCartney had died in a car accident and an imposter had taken his place. The Man in The Iron Mask scenario, and what relevance it had as to whether this group existed or not was a very odd argument to put forward. It was as if we talk about this random "non" subject we are being very "transparent" and you will believe us. Well, that would be a big no from me, I didn't. And like millions of others, I no longer watch BBC news because it is incredibly biased, and I have witnessed far too many interviews that would be construed as harassment and bullying.

It is not just the BBC who is doing this it is very widespread and anyone who points out a flaw in an argument is attacked behind the guise of decency and fairness, it's vile and it needs to stop.

People such as J.K Rowling, Jordan Peterson, Nigel Farage, Donald Trump, Piers Morgan, Mel Gibson, Maya Forstater, Kathleen Stock, Alan Bates and The Sub Post Masters, Rev

Dr Bernard Randall, Katharine Birbalsingh, Sharon Davis and many more like them have been discredited, threatened with death, rape and maiming, denied bank accounts, ostracised, accused of theft, lied to, sacked and dissuaded from telling the truth, but yet they all still bravely speak out. Regardless of whether you agree with some of them or not, please try and imagine if the boot was on the other foot. And it was you who was being silenced, threatened or was the recipient of actual bodily harm, it's not remotely acceptable in a so called civilized society.

News channels such as GB News and Talk TV struggle because of a lack of funding due to a shortage of advertisers. I expect many large companies would love to promote their goods on these channels but are told if they do so that they will lose far larger and more lucrative contracts. GB News always allows both sides of the debate to be heard, which is correct in a society which is supposedly democratic.

Because of the way things are going I no longer watch the news on a daily basis. Not because I am burying my head in the sand, but because I know the score and things are sadly going to get far worse. However, when I do want to have an update with regards to what is going on I watch GB News. And I hope that they will continue to speak for the ordinary people who are in the majority. Who know precisely what is going on and what lies beneath and behind all the corruption greed and elitism which is currently rife in this world.

What can we do about all of these elitist and secretive groups? In all honesty, nothing at all as they are very far reaching and have their fingers in far too many pies. Although it does not affect us physically what they are all doing is far worse than any viral pandemic. They have always existed and there will always be good guys, bad guys and those in between who are indifferent. All we can do is neutralise their input, stick together and hope that the indifferent wake up and see what is going on and join forces with all of the good guys. So be very careful what you tread in when you venture outside of your home and when you deal with others. Always remain kind, loving, brave but also be street wise and smart, and do not engage with angry, bitter, cruel or haughty people and hold your own counsel.

And whether this is going to happen in my lifetime or many years further down the line. Never entertain the idea of having a chip inserted into your body. Which will be used to pay for items without the need for carrying cash or a credit card. Even if you are threatened to do so, please don't, because if you do you will become a part of something that is irreversible and your card will quite literally be spiritually marked.

Being able to speak on an appropriate and fair non biased platform makes people listen and take notice, and this must always be done to fight injustice that affects all colours, all genders and all ages for many different reasons. So many forms of injustice that all must be highlighted, and no group should ever claim that their suffering has more gravitas than another. It simply is not the case and creates further division, the implication is that another groups pain and suffering is irrelevant or minimal in comparison to one highlighted group is completely unjust.

The inference that people with a white skin are "privileged" according to the Critical Race Theory, is yet another form of bias without basis. Hypothetically if a middle-class white male was initially from a working-class background and was a victim of sexual abuse as a child but has fought his entire life to overcome his ordeal and is currently successful. I do not believe it fair to say that he is in a position of "privilege" if compared to a person of colour who is of precisely the same standing and has not been a victim of any form of abuse. Whatever colour we are it is not of our choosing; subsequently skin colour should not be used as leverage to achieve goals. Dumbing down another's shining light by saying that it was automatically "given" without knowing a person's actual back story is not something that should be promoted in any way shape or form.

I am truly saddened that the words of Martin Luther King Junior have been lost on a minority element of people who do not remotely understand the word equality. Which is a level playing field for all, it does not ignore another's suffering and nor does it utilize differences spoken about by those with an agenda to stymie others with equally valid points. Martin Luther King Jnr spoke at a time when black people were treated appallingly. The injustice, he witnessed and experienced enabled him to speak with passion, clarity, sadness and frustration, but also with a great deal of hope. Throughout his speech he spoke of his wish for unity and respect between black and white citizens. And also, that his four little children would not be judged by the colour of their skin but by the content of their character. And this applies to every one of us who lives on this earth.

I am not an academic and I cannot write a speech like Martin Luther King Jnr but as a fellow Christian INFJ who lives in a world which currently has far too many troublemakers in it, I have precisely the same need to voice my concerns. I am tired of listening to people from both sides who are equally determined to cause division and hatred and constantly pick at a scab which is never allowed time to heal.

Constantly referring to historical injustice as a default "fallback" position, does not allow past wounds to heal, and nor does historical abuse make all within a group a victim who automatically gets reverence, simply for existing. Our real focus should be on the many pockets of people of all ethnicities currently suffering around the world for many different reasons, who really need our help.

The word diversity is frequently used, and I feel it is not all encompassing and has become polarized. When we think of the word we tend to think of an inclusion-based dynamic that involves ensuring that there is sufficient representation of minority groups. The word by its very definition does not relate solely to particular groups. It is a general term which encompasses many things and not solely skin colour. There are many more aspects to a person's make up: their individual personality traits, physical appearance, spiritual beliefs, a person's unique work ethic, their political viewpoints and the list goes on and on. If a group of people were randomly selected by a neutral source and placed in a room together, the diversity criteria would be met by all the people within the room as they are all unique individuals.

Just as I have never thought about ethnicity and feel we all should be judged solely by our character and how we treat our fellow man, I have always felt precisely the same about gender. Ultimately, we are all souls that simply inhabit a body for a very short period, and what our body looks like or represents is of little importance. We are all unique physically and it is wonderful that we are. I personally do not understand this need to describe our entire identity solely based on our sexual preferences or our genitalia. I would like to think that if anyone had to describe me, my character traits and actions would be discussed, and not what I identify as.

So many words and descriptions that we must all accept without question, and yet the definition and description of a woman is incredibly difficult. An answer which is simple and based solely on science and biology, but a response based on this fact is met with derision. I should not be made to feel ashamed for being a sex that was assigned to me and is merely a sequence of biological contributory factors that had a scientific outcome. How on earth am I supposed to describe myself in this insane world? A vessel with blood, major organs, a functioning central nervous system, a defunct reproductive system that was once able to bear children, an ordinary brain that is not receptive to BS and is therefore irrelevant in today's bonkers society.

I cannot believe how self-centred humanity is becoming, prioritizing words and descriptions, over far more serious matters such as war. A beautiful little Downs Syndrome girl walking with her mother in the Ukraine pushing her pushchair whilst chatting to her mum. Smiling regardless of her location and circumstances, and four minutes later blown up. Seriously are we all so self-absorbed that identity politics are of far more importance than war crimes?

Sadly, most of the problems that are currently in the world are caused by people that hijack causes and say that they represent them, when often they do not and merely have an agenda. The problem is unless we question the motives of people who do this, they succeed in causing further division. Stonewall does not represent all who are LGBTQ+ and The Black Lives Matter movement does not represent all black or people of colour they both represent the minority. But as they have influence over various groups usually based on fear or payment, they can control narratives, and this is extremely dangerous.

We must remember that there are millions of people within these groups who feel precisely the same as us, and they are just as concerned and frustrated by what they are witnessing. We need to stand united as a group, one which has unbreakable bonds that are formed on truth and love, for these things will always trump those which are steeped in greed, ego and hatred. This is a time of change, and it can only go one way if we are to survive. If we do nothing in as little as ten years, there will be even more changes and our society will become almost unrecognisable.

We have become incredibly fearful of speaking out about the behaviour of a minority element of people of colour, and this has been used very much against us. It has enabled some to continue to break the law without reproach, they have a green light to abuse, and it is absolutely disgusting. An example of which applies to the Rochdale gang who repeatedly raped those poor teenage girls for years. If it hadn't been for two courageous ladies who received flack for speaking the "actual truth" many more children and teenagers would have been gang raped, which is beyond sickening. Once again, I will reiterate that we all should be judged on our actions and how we treat others, our skin colour has nothing to do with accountability or addressing a problem. Perpetrators of such heinous crimes invariably pull the Human Rights card to avoid deportation. The people assessing their status need to imagine themselves laying on a filthy mattress, petrified waiting for the door to open again, but of course they do not as they have no ability to put themselves in those poor girls' shoes.

Political correctness is the order of the day, a weapon designed to silence anyone when an argument cannot be refuted. A loaded gun which is often pulled by people who profess to being kind and caring and hide behind the generic term of liberalism. The dictionary definition of this word is " willingness to respect or accept behaviour or opinions different from one's own, openness to new ideas". A perfect ideology if implemented, and there are truly millions of people with strongly held liberal values in this world who fully own this definition and deservedly so. However, the word holds precisely no gravitas and is hollow if adopted by any person or organization that bullies another simply for holding a differing opinion.

Repression of thoughts and control of another's freethinking leads to untold damage to a person's mental health and will ultimately lead to pent up anger that will either turn inwardly and cause disease or outwardly and cause violent acts. In the past certain topics were not discussed if you felt someone had an opposing opinion, but if you felt comfortable enough with a person to engage in a debate and no common ground was found, the end of the conversation was always "Let's just agree to disagree" how simple is that a mutual respect for one another's differing views.

People who follow these misguided principles, or who worship at the altar of self will always attack and they can be incredibly vitriolic and venomous. However, millions of us are very firmly in "the know" and we are all fighting back. I am not alone but nestled within a very strong army on a very perfectly planned mission, one which is based in love and truth, and we will always win. We do not need to resort to underhand tactics, and nor do we need to threaten or bully anyone, we will just leave the enemy to their own devices and gradually they will hoist themselves on their own petards. Every single cruel word or attack on any of us will simply confirm the truth of our words and add more strings to our arsenal of primed bow's. Which are backed up by loving arrows of truth that will fire directly at an enemy who uses tactics which are all to easily recognized. We do not need to use telescopic sight on our bows as the enemy is obvious and it is parading around smugly and is well within target range. In fact, if it gets any closer it will be on some people's backs. Not to worry though although the blinded cannot see what is in their midst, we can.

Song: Silent Running Mike and The Mechanics

Zombie by The Cranberries

I believe COVID was manufactured by using both the Sars and Mers strain of the virus to make a third mutation. Aimed to be a biological weapon to destabilise the world's economy at some point, and it has worked because most Countries have been financially crippled by it. I am not sure whether it was meant to be released or it was an accident, however the Chinese New Year spread it round the world like wildfire. If it was intentional, it would have been the perfect strike. Xi Jinping has openly laid out his plans for world domination, which he hopes to achieve by 2050, which is beyond hideous. Building a virology centre, near an ancient and established wet market was I believe no coincidence, as any incidents would then be blamed on a recognized potential source of zoonotic viruses, the perfect alibi. If I am completely wrong and it did miraculously come from a pangolin or some other such strange species. The CCP are still culpable because if they knew the severity of the virus and still allowed its citizens to leave China and travel globally, it is akin to serial manslaughter.

There is much good in this beautiful world, but I have always known that there is sadly the complete opposite. It is not nice and nor should we clutter our minds with it or give it any credence. However, we should not be naive to its existence, because it will creep up on us and bite us firmly on our derrieres if we are. A quote attributed to Edmund Burke could not be any more apt "All that is required for evil to triumph, is for good men to do nothing."

In Brazil mass graves were being hastily dug whilst heartbroken relatives were unable to give a respectful and dignified send off for their loved ones, which was heartbreaking to witness. Whilst over here many people were whinging that they hadn't been on their usual hols, couldn't go out for a beer, RIP haircuts, manicures and the Big Mac all of sufficient gravitas to induce trauma. Many of the staff on the worlds COVID wards will need trauma counselling and have PTSD. Children will have been emotionally damaged by what they have seen, and the restriction of their normal childhood movements will have affected them dramatically. It is incredibly sad, and I hope that there is a support network or literature available to them to enable them to heal. Cancer patients who had their chemo or radio therapy delayed, important diagnoses missed due to GP's not having face to face consultations, suicides due to the lack of access to a mental health professional as well as lockdown isolation exacerbating depression, and people losing their homes and jobs all because of this terrible virus. My sympathy is for all these groups, and to all those that lost a loved one during this pandemic. And not the father who felt traumatized that he couldn't take his children on their yearly skiing trip to The Alps. I nearly kicked the TV screen in on hearing this heartbreaking tale of woe!

Song: I Me Mine by The Beatles

Many weapons are used to destabilize our Country and human beings are also used by those who wish us ill. They see a weakness and spot a loophole and utilize it to the absolute max. And this is precisely what is happening with regards to the thousands of illegal immigrants that are coming to our shores. And yes, I do believe that some are genuinely seeking asylum. And without question some of the people in the boats will be unwilling passengers who have been forced to come over and will be forced into prostitution or be modern day slaves or drug runners. And many of the children will be passed into the hands of paedophile gangs which is truly heartbreaking. These people are humans just like us and we should always be accommodating to genuine asylum seekers and vulnerable women and children.

But as we all know the majority of people crossing the Channel are young fighting age men, who have discarded any paperwork that identifies their true nationality, and identity. Which of course also removes the possibility of checking any criminal records and activity. Would we allow all Russian Chinese and North Korean citizens to come over on dinghies, and enter our Country with no questions asked or verified? The bottom line is the threat to our Country's national security has never been so high.

So what can be done about this situation, to be honest I think we must no longer concentrate on processing those who have been here for months. The horse has long since bolted and we must focus our attention on each boat that arrives in our waters. And this means processing and vetting immediately on an offshore facility. I cannot for the life of me understand how a simple interview process which is regularly conducted by airport border security staff in a few hours, does not apply in this situation. They act expediently and the person is sent back on a flight immediately to where they came from. Of course this is a problem because they have come from France. But surely a flight to their Country from whence they came would be a reasonable solution. Unless they were a clear threat to the planes security they could fly alone. Surely there are Border Control Laws that can be enforced. If there isn't then there is no need for a passport everything is fluid and we can all live wherever we want in the world. None of it makes any sense, and it makes me wonder whether some within our Governments both past and present are just paying us lip service when they say they agree that the situation is unacceptable. Perhaps they actually want a break down in society, leaving the door open for someone they just happen to know to come and take control of the situation and our Country.

So having circular conversations as to why this is a dangerous situation will continue to fall on deaf ears. I have formed my personal opinion on this matter with regards to infrastructure, statistics, security, equality, meritocracy, personal experience and also witnessing behaviour that is not acceptable within our society. Although human beings are essentially all the same, the fact is our societal and moral values differ tremendously. The layout of the land, the temperature, the food we eat, our ancestors' religions and beliefs, all shape us to fit in first and foremostly with the area in which we were born. There is no right, there is no wrong and it is precisely the way it is supposed to be. Some Countries cultural and societal values are incredibly similar to ours and there is no friction. Whilst others have cultural differences that can become points of contention, if forced upon the indigenous population. To co-exist there must be tolerance on both sides, but the onus should be placed on the incomer to adapt. Many do so and hats off to them, because I would do precisely the same.

When in Rome do as the Romans do, and if I was unable to adapt and conform, I would leave.

I wish it was a happy world and we all could get along with one another, but I am a realist and there will always be extremes of opinions. Throughout history this has always resulted in the pendulum swinging too far to one side. Which of course invokes opposition, and then it will rapidly swing straight over to the other side, without pausing for a second in the middle. Which is where I want the pendulum to stop and remain, but it is highly unlikely. Without having billions of little islands in which we could all choose the ideal people to share it with, there will always be problems, it is the order of things. And until there is divine intervention on the grandest of scales, when some serious spiritual butt is kicked things will remain the same.

Globalism and multiculturism is the dream of those with individual agendas who want to rule the world. Without any added pressures from external sources, we are already fighting amongst ourselves. And only a few groups of people are listening to the ordinary man on the street. It is very much do as we say and not as we do. Anything that is not in our back yard, it is your problem. And if you dare to say you are unhappy about it, we will call you a racist, fascist or bigot. Inflammatory words that are insulting and could not be further from the truth. But yet denial is futile because you are then accused of having unconscious bias. Akin to a murder trial when an innocent man pleads not guilty, he is given a life sentence because he has unconscious guilt. It is all becoming absolutely ridiculous.

I truthfully have never felt the need to think about class as you should know by now, I believe we are all the same. I didn't want to think otherwise but life has shown me just how big the class divide is. We rarely have a platform and if we are given the opportunity to speak, at times it smacks of tokenism. Listening to an academic or writer speak words that we may have said ten years before, as if they invented the wheel, really presses all of my buttons. It's like being in an echo chamber, whilst they profess to speak for us. Some do and I am discerning enough to know the difference. Cockiness and smugness is just annoying. Passionate, humble and erudite is the way to get people on side.

Historical figures and events are being censored and cancelled to suit by a minority element which is beyond disturbing. Historical events both positive and negative ground us as human beings, we have reference points that we can learn from. It is also comforting to know that the world has evolved in some respects for the better but also for the worse. Trying to obliterate the past takes our identity away and erodes our sense of self. George Orwell's uncanny intuition with regards to a minority element potentially using 1984 as a manual to wreak mayhem, uncertainty and division is eerily accurate he quoted " The most effective way to destroy people is to deny and obliterate their own understanding of their history." All the crazy stuff that is currently being fed to us comes from so many sources for various reasons. Countries that want world domination will target groups through social media and technology in general. I am without doubt that new ideologies that cause doubt, confusion and division originate from these Countries.

Their citizens have no real freedom and are fed lies by the state-controlled media. Whilst over here rules are not enforced and our heads are full of irrelevant nonsense, small toxic seeds which they have gradually planted over the years. I am sure this is not coincidental and without doubt the leaders of these Countries are laughing at our stupidity, naivety and greed. Educational establishments who have received funding from China have made an awful mistake, as failure to implement "recommendations" from their generous donors leaves individuals in charge of universities and such like wide open to blackmail. Students most likely will have been fed destabilizing information because of undue influence. Not all will be indoctrinated, however it is terrifying if you think about it.

I sincerely hope that this obsession with social media and reading a bloody smartphone 24/7 becomes outdated and there is a dramatic about face. Mobile phones are without doubt as addictive as smoking and drinking. People's noses pressed against the screen in abject terror that their latest post did not receive. Crossing roads and paying minimal attention to the traffic or walking among the most beautiful of scenery and paying no attention to their surroundings. Seriously the sky is stunning, this planet is beautiful there is so much beauty around us, focusing on yourself constantly is unhealthy.

I truly don't understand the personal need to constantly self-promote, some people who already have a public platform seek more and more attention and re- post material that is already out there for the world to see. What is wrong with liking yourself truly from within, and not from a point of extreme vanity or arrogance?   It does take time and believe me I know it has been one hell of a journey. Strangers likes mean diddly squat, first base is to truly like yourself and if you have friends and family that love you too, that is more than sufficient.

Much of the worlds problems are related to inflated ego's and people like you and I are often pushed out of the equation. Of course we cannot all speak at once, because the clarity and tone of our words will not resonate and resound with others. But our voices must not be discouraged and dismissed immediately as irrelevant. Especially during this pivotal time in history. I know that if we are complacent now, that we will live to regret it. I would rather try and fail, than to sit with my head buried in the sand.

For anyone like me without a celebrity status or political platform who have their own voice, their own mind and care passionately about this world and the beautiful people in it. You may or may not agree with what I have said, but if we all want a safe and beautiful world, with love at its core, and ego's left right at the door, we can still turn this around, but only if we work together.

Song Choices:

Sweet Harmony by The Beloved

With a Little Luck by Wings

Something Inside So Strong by Labi Sifre

I am What I am from La Cage aux Folles

THE BEACH 13

I Believe in Angels

No surprises that a song has a very direct and poignant connection to my one and only angel sighting. The song and the video combined are a must watch if you want to see my unusual angel's appearance. No wings I am afraid, not 7ft tall with long white hair, wearing white robes and twinkly blue eyes. My angel was a doppelganger of the actor who was the main character in Energy 52's Cafe Del Mar video.

I heard this track for the very first time with Ross who was a bit of a poser. He DJ'd part time in clubs and loved old school trance. He was in a good mood and had rung me to see whether I would like to go to the coast for a walk with him. He picked me up in his white beamer and put some music on. This track came on and I adored it, it had a very steady beat which went on for quite some time which I found almost hypnotic.

Ross then said, "Sis it's going to kick in now are you ready?" and after a few more beats it did, big time and it was exhilarating. The tracks entire beat resonated with me, the repetitive steady part and then the kick arse section that not many people get to see. We spent a lovely few hours together and talked about life, and many other things. We were on the same page on that day, and I will never forget it.

Although I have eventually reached a point of very peaceful acceptance with regards to not having any contact with my family of origin. I play the track sometimes for Ross and me, with a wish and a prayer that one day I will see him again, if not in this life it will be the next. This has brought tears to my eyes, not too bad, I have only had three wobbles so far!

A few years ago, I was completely exhausted with a situation at home "The Dilemma", and I was feeling thoroughly disillusioned. I had ventured into the dreaded Pity Party Saloon and felt like staying there for a while. I was extremely stressed and had been to see a doctor, I have only ever been three times in my life with regards to stress, and it has always been caused by external circumstances. I broke down in tears and let it all out, I just needed to speak to someone face to face very briefly who was not in the mix which did help. I was tired of always trying hard to do the right thing and always losing and being amidst mental health issues and personality disorders.

Looking at the sea and walking on the beach usually lifts my mood and makes me very conscious of how very small and insignificant we all are in the grander scheme of things. So, I went to the local beach with our beautiful collie and was throwing the ball into the sea for her to fetch. Whilst having a

"Why me" discussion with the Big Man upstairs. Why when I always told the truth did I lose? Why when I had such strong faith did, I continually have to fight? I told him I was sick and tired of fighting and pleaded with him "Please I need help, please help me". I honestly have never felt so defeated. I was on the point of giving up mentally, not physically though, and I had no intention of harming myself.

I was standing in the water and crying, and suddenly in my peripheral vision to my left, a shape caught my attention. It was only what I can describe as an orange bobbing balloon which was moving along sideways rather than floating upwards. I felt compelled to go towards a particular spot on the beach, as if I was on the end of a fishing line and I was being reeled in. I said to Baby Girl" come on we must go over here" And off we went on our unplanned detour which was only about 500 yards from where we were playing.

When I reached the point at the bottom of the cliffs edge, the rock formation was in a crescent shape, so it looked like a cove. Immediately I felt like I had walked through an invisible porthole into what felt like an outdoor church. An incredible stillness descended upon me. I instantly felt settled and peaceful, and my hopeless feeling had vanished. I knew it was an opportunity that I was being given, to never doubt my faith or Gods existence. I stood in awe and soaked up this wonderful, peaceful feeling, and I thanked God for showing me that it was all going to be ok. There was a cave like entrance to the left, only large enough for a couple of people to sit in. And a collection of rocks in front of it that seemed to be perfectly laid out. In the middle of the rock formation was positioned the largest rock that looked like a natural font, and it had a few inches of water in it.

Baby Girl had plonked herself down and I had an opportunity to stay still and enjoy the peace that I had been given and to say a prayer. With a piece of driftwood, I drew a big circle in the sand and proceeded to write all the names of the kind and decent people in my life who I felt needed a prayer of protection and love, and I said a prayer for them all, and one for me. I thanked God for helping me that day and for all that he had done for me throughout my life, that had enabled me to always retain my faith regardless of the trouble in my life and in the world.

I stood in front of my personal font and dipped my cupped hand into it to collect some of the salt water. I then walked to the circle and sprinkled some of the sea water over it. And finally, I collected a little more sea water from the natural font and put some on Baby Girls head whilst saying God Bless and then some on my own. After my impromptu personal service, I felt an incredible peace and stillness, one that I had never felt before.

Once more out of the corner of my left eye something seemed to be materializing from the rock face. The shape solidified and standing no more than twenty feet away from me was a very serene looking bald man with dark glasses. He had a slim athletic build, a black tee shirt and very light brown jeans. I stared at him, and he smiled very sweetly at me, and so I smiled back. I thought oh my goodness he must have been watching me all this time, how embarrassing, he probably thinks I am a proper weirdo, why didn't I notice him?

He began to walk away towards the beach's car park. He was walking in a way that I had only seen once before, in the Cafe Del Mar video, with an almost perfect gait, and with purpose and determination, however his movements seemed effortless. He almost reached the brow of a small hill and promptly disappeared; I knew instantly that he was an angel. I try to rationalise things and often doubt myself far too much. And I am sure that if I had seen some sort of ethereal looking angel, I would have thought it a trick of the light and not taken it seriously.

It was no coincidence that the big man upstairs had sent me my own Cafe Del Mar Angel. When I went home, I immediately played it on You Tube and had forgotten that there was a section in the video when he was walking along a cliff face. What a blinding result, I had only stayed in Pity Party Plaza for a couple of drinks, thank goodness it was a brief stay because the Chardonnay sucked and was beginning to taste a little bitter.

Songs: If God Was One of Us by Joan Osborne

Solsbury Hill by Peter Gabriel

And for my brother Ross a song that he loved...

She Sells Sanctuary by The Cult

ROOM 14

Judy's Beloved

And now on to something completely different, a chapter about workplace bullying...

The company I worked for was at the time a great place to work, and what happened was not a reflection of the companies' standards or ethics as a rule. This incident relates to one serial workplace bully, a very inexperienced store manager and an area manager who wasn't too keen on anyone who had an opinion.

I worked in a dispensary and various courses had to be completed to ensure that you are safe dispensing drugs, and you understand their use and how they work within the body. At the level I had reached I was able to give advice to customers regarding certain health problems and symptoms that were more complex than medicine counter queries.

Pharmacists are always available to talk and give patients advice, but if the matter is straight forward you act as a buffer. This allows them to concentrate on whether you have issued the correct drug to the correct patient and that the drugs on the prescription have no interactions and are safe to be issued.

Because I am a neat freak and was good at biology at school, it was the perfect position for me. I was proficient at my job and good with the customers. I had good time management skills, and when I left that branch, two people were put in the dispensary to cope with the workload I routinely did alone. I am pretty average at most things I do, but when I like doing something I do apply myself 100% and this I did in my role.

I had worked for the company for many years and never had any issues with any staff members or management. I was just a head down grafter who thoroughly enjoyed my job. It is extremely important that you have a good working relationship with the pharmacist, one which is very much based on trust. I had worked with many pharmacists, regular ones, managers and locums over the years and there were never any problems. We would have a chat and a laugh if we ever had a minute spare, the rest of the time it was very much task focused work. No trouble at all, until Pollyanna's arrival.

I chose the name Pollyanna as she looked like a 1970's chocolate box model. Picture perfect, twinkly blue eyes, long brunette hair, Colegate smile and all seemingly very wholesome. Pollyanna was based at another store, and I had been working with a lovely female locum for a few months, as the stores permanent pharmacist had left to work for another company. We got on extremely well and had a good working relationship, she was a very experienced pharmacist, and the dispensary was running very efficiently.

One day a pharmacist Nina who worked at the store where Pollyanna was based came over to cover the locum's lunch and day said, "I am so pleased to be over here for a bit Kim". I asked her why and she replied that it was awful where she was working, and Pollyanna was causing a tremendous number of problems at the branch. One of whom was a young quiet girl who had "lost it" after something inappropriate and cruel had been said to her. And had walked out and spent the whole afternoon wandering round the town in floods of tears.

Pollyanna had also called a customer a spastic when they had questioned her abilities. And had displayed aggressive behaviour by forcefully slamming a door on a colleague who was walking through. Nina said that she had never worked in such an awful environment and the whole dynamic at the branch was being affected by the new arrival, and she had "never come across anyone so strange in her entire life".

Pollyanna did come to my branch occasionally to cover the locum's lunch, and she was always helpful and very low key when she came. However, the situation soon came to a head at the store where she was based. A Mexican stand-off had occurred between Pollyanna and all the staff who had been badly affected by her behaviour. They said that they were going to leave if the manager didn't address the current situation. Subsequently Pollyanna walked out and came to our store to work as the permanent pharmacist.

The staff at Pollyanna's old branch were extremely concerned about me working alone with her and told me that they were there for me if I needed them. However, they thought that she wouldn't do anything to me because I was older, and they knew that I would speak out if something was not right. I presumed after what had happened Pollyanna would reign herself in and not put in a repeat performance, I was so wrong she in fact upped the ante.

On arrival she brought cream cakes for all the staff, which is nice if you are in a small team but buying 35+ seemed a little OTT. She also seemed a little manic and far too familiar with the customers, who were clearly very uncomfortable. Also, some of the pharmaceutical advice she was giving was not in line with company protocol, it was very much her take and interpretation of what she personally thought to be correct.

Things slowly crept in with regards to her behaviour towards me, she would routinely question the most rudimentary things I said, and seemed furious when customers came in to ask for me personally or acknowledged me. She would push herself in front of me and launch an inappropriate charm offensive on them, imagine a car salesman and double it.

There were around twenty regular customers who I had known for many years, and we had very friendly but professionally appropriate conversations. I knew their medical history and their personal medical needs, and I always ensured when a prescription was due that they received their meds on time. Somewhat strangely Pollyanna decided to write Christmas cards only to them with a personal message from her, which she sent to their home addresses. If a customer signs up online for a service, it was permissible for the company to use their address, but it most definitely was not company policy to use a patient's medical record for anything other than the safe supply of medicine, and most certainly not for personal promotion.

Copious cans of red bull were stacked at the rear of dispensary her pyramid as she called it, and strange rambling statements were being written in the rear of the private prescription book. Which is normally only used to log a prescription the cost and verbatim what the prescriber had written. It is a legal logbook and not designed for statements such as " I have a sore throat and have taken an ibuprofen at 7.35 am and therefore I feel like my judgement is impaired and I cannot be held fully responsible ". I had never seen a pharmacist use the record like that and I began to think something was terribly amiss. A well-respected colleague who worked in a role appertaining to finances and security had come into dispensary and seen Pollyanna place her purse into the controlled drug safe, she was using it as her personal locker. From a store security aspect and with regards to pharmaceutical protocol and procedures this was also not permitted. There must be a legitimate reason for you to open the safe due to the nature of the drugs within it. I had not been aware of this, and my colleague immediately told our manager, but no action was taken, and she couldn't understand why.

After a while I felt it necessary to have a chat with my manager Judy with regards to Pollyanna's unpleasant and odd behaviour towards me and I told her that this had been a modus operandi in her previous store. I also explained that I was a little concerned that the company's rules and pharmacy standard operating procedures were not being adhered to. And explained that unlike the shop a pharmacy was governed by strict legislation which could not be deviated from without serious consequences.

Judy was fine and listened and told me that I was extremely good at my job, and she thought I could deal with it all without her intervention. She had no knowledge of pharmacy law or protocol and therefore made the wrong assumption that in my role it would be the norm to question or challenge their senior. Judy was not au fait with dispensary protocol and had not managed a store with a dispensary. She was as far as I thought a good manager and appreciated how hard I worked.

And often used to pop into the dispensary and say hello and ask me how things were going. One day she called me away from the pharmacy and said, "Kim I was listening to some advice you gave a customer and I feel that you are better at your job than a lot of pharmacists, is there any way I can help you become one"? I was flattered but explained "It doesn't work like that I would have to go to university for several years and would not be able to work" I thanked her though for her kind words. That was the vibe of the relationship we had, but that was soon to be turned completely on its head.

Her daily visits abruptly stopped, and she barely spoke to me, I was initially perplexed but was without doubt that Pollyanna had been doing a hatchet job on me. A younger colleague who I had always been friends with and had helped with her dispenser training became very frosty and monosyllabic for no reason at all. A newly appointed male team leader was chatting to me about something that needed to be done, and out of the blue he called me very obstructive. The knives were out, but luckily most people knew me very well, and whatever lies she was peddling, barely touched the sides, it could have been far worse.

Pollyanna's unpleasant behaviour was intensifying with each passing day. She was extremely erratic and rude to me when no one was within earshot. However, as soon as any management were in the vicinity, she transformed immediately into the most wonderful and kind and considerate person you could ever wish to meet. Some regular customers had disappeared, and the remaining ones told me on the QT that they thought she was very creepy and odd. I listened but didn't respond as it would not have been professional to be rude about a colleague.

At this time there was a Customer Survey running where you may win a few pounds if you reported how your store visit went. These were issued randomly with a separate receipt when you served someone. Pollyanna began to get repeated ones, I had only a couple because most people can't be bothered to complete them, but at least mine were genuine. Pollyanna had about twelve in a couple of months, most of which had very particular personal details and very gushy over descriptive language. Comments such as" I had a wonderful experience when I came in store today, the pharmacist I think her name was Pollyanna had long dark brown hair was tall and came from another country, she gave me the most incredible advice and I felt so reassured after speaking to her". It's a miracle they didn't know her bra and shoe sizes as well! Several other staff members noticed the same and I know that a couple of them questioned their validity. However, Pollyanna was issued with an award for giving the best customer service throughout the entire region off the back of them, A photo opportunity for the stores staff magazine took place which naturally I kept well out of view from.

Every prescription I dispensed she "over checked" every single item however rudimentary would be scrutinized for an eternity. A box of paracetamol she would count and recount in-between staring at me in absolute disgust. My years of proven experience and certification counted for nothing. It was a very clear attempt to make me feel uncomfortable and an attempt to undermine my competency. I began to feel on edge it worked, however not once did she ever find an error, which really annoyed her. This was admittedly incredibly difficult as dispensing under such pressure is not wise as when you are overly tired or stressed mistakes can happen.

If I had a day off the minimum amount of work was done and any call backs were left in a large pile for me to dispense. The first time it happened I asked the trainee dispenser what had happened, as little to no work had been done and the dispensary was in a state of disarray. She told me that Pollyanna had told her not to worry about any outstanding prescriptions when I had a day off and to catch up on her training. She clearly wanted me to start the day at a disadvantage, so after a day off I would come in early whilst there were no customers to catch up, which really annoyed her. Once I had dispensed about twenty prescriptions before her arrival and was completing the final one, and she said very illogically "Why didn't you do this one first, that is what I wanted you to do".

I was working twice as hard in the dispensary, which was very busy without any extra tasks. The company although relatively professional was always trying to save money and if it could utilize employees that worked hardest to save costs it would happily do so. In dispensaries it is important that things run safely and there was enough cover to do all the tasks. There was a colour code with regards to dispensary staff resources and it was no surprise the stores dispensary was often on the wrong end of the colour spectrum. Under normal circumstances I didn't mind being so busy, and it was simply because I was able to prioritize my time effectively that the workload was achievable. However, with the unnecessary added tasks and bullying to deal with it was becoming too much. I was physically sick a few times before work and felt my anxiety levels increase daily. I had a permanent dull headache and felt unusually tearful and generally unwell.

Once again, I told Judy that I was suffering like the staff in Pollyanna's previous store. And her half-hearted unprofessional attempt to sort the mess out, was a discussion in the consultation booth, which was so tiny that Pollyanna was almost sitting on my lap. Whilst Judy talked a load of irrelevant and utter nonsense about personalities and teamwork.

I had noticed her and Pollyanna together a few times looking at posh skincare lines and giggling, it wasn't hard to work out, why Judy had been blanking me, they had become friends rather than colleagues. BTW I'm calling her Judy as it reflected her image, all boucle suit and pumps and an eager beaver attitude, not after Judy Finnegan, who I have always liked and loved her book, Eloise.

On the morning's car journey into work, I used to put on the theme from the film Gladiator to motivate me, and in my uniform trouser pocket I put a copy of my favourite poem "If" by Rudyard Kipling which made me feel stronger. I just didn't want to go into work, and as per usual music and literature helped me face my daily ordeal.

On arrival into work one morning Judy rung down to dispensary. I answered, and she sounded extremely shirty and irritated, and summoned me upstairs to see her immediately. I went to her office, and she curtly told me to sit down, and then proceeded to tell me that Pollyanna had rung her at home the previous evening and was apparently extremely distressed. She proceeded to rant at me and told me she was utterly disgusted that I was not supporting such a wonderful pharmacist, and how lucky the store was to have her.

She told me that I was extremely lazy, and Pollyanna was doing all the work. My attitude was completely unprofessional and what the hell was the matter with me? Finally, she said that just because I missed my "beloved " regular pharmacist, with a definite inference that it was more than a working relationship, that it was absolutely no reason or excuse to be so surly, lazy and unprofessional. I sat in complete and utter shock and then began to cry, to which she snapped at me to stop it, and to get out of her office.

I immediately ran to the only place of sanctuary in the building the ladies' toilets, shaken to the core and trying desperately to pull myself together. Whilst wiping my eyes trying to make my face look less like a combination of panda and roadkill, and in walked Pollyanna. My composure had finally left me there was no point in hiding it she had won. However, I still turned round and looked her directly in the eye and held my chin up. Truthfully my mum's final gloating smirk was amateurish in comparison, the only way I can truthfully describe her demeanour was one of ice cold chilling gleeful contempt.

I had to speak to someone in authority before I left for home and spoke to a professional female team leader with regards to what had just happened. I explained that a lovely Saturday staff member who was at university training to be a pharmacist, had left because of the way Pollyanna had treated him. On one of my rare Saturdays off she had insulted him for no reason, and when I next saw him, he told me he never wanted to be left alone with her again, and had handed his notice in. He was one of the nicest people you could ever wish to meet and was a top student in his course, it was such a shame. The team leader listened and was very kind, and I told her that I felt so ill that I was going home, and probably would have to resign, if nothing was done to address the situation.

I went home and my beautiful collie sat with me on the sofa as I sobbed my heart out. Bless her she was always really loving but only ever did this once. She managed to place her front left leg on my shoulder like she was putting a little arm round me. I felt a little better after my hug and decided I was going to ring the union which I did. I told the rep everything, not in detail just the cold hard facts. He listened patiently whilst I relayed countless incidents. When I had finished, he said "Kim this is one of the worst cases of workplace bullying I have ever heard of, do not resign, people should not be able to get away with this. Write all of it down, and you are going to have to lodge an official grievance against both your manager and the pharmacist". Which I did, I hope you can imagine it was factual and precise on both counts, I listed the main events, witnesses to some of the events, how her actions had made me feel and referred also to pharmacy protocol and law.

It was factual and concise, and in Pollyanna's case 5 A4 sheets long (both sides). Five employees from the previous store said that they would happily be witnesses to clarify her behaviour. and if necessary, would speak at a Tribunal to support me. Nina the pharmacist was one of the five which was incredibly brave of her. She was extremely astute and intuitive and once said to me "Kim I am as sure as I can be that she is a narcissist".

I was interviewed for each grievance and simply told the truth. With regards to Pollyanna, I was interviewed by the Regional Head Pharmacist and a supervisor, and my friend Sara came along with me for support. I strongly felt that they both knew I was telling the truth but was fully aware that the Area Manager would ultimately have the final word, I should have felt confident, but I didn't.

Pollyanna had the perfect companion during her interview, Cleo a manager of a tiny local branch. She had the most terrible reputation with regards to bullying people and staff turnover was at such a level it should have been investigated. I worked at her branch for ten days and it was a terrible experience, she behaved more like a dictator than a retail manager. The staff were petrified of her mood swings and her reputation was well known throughout the entire area. She was eventually fired for gross misconduct, stealing from her store, a perfect supportive shoulder for Pollyanna.

With regards to Judy, I was interviewed by the Regional Investigation Branch officer who was an ex-police officer, and a Store Manager from a neutral branch. This I did feel far more confident about as the Investigation Officer had been involved in a serious incident, which I had reported to the police, and I was told later that my suspicions had been correct. I knew that he would be bang on point and would not be swayed in the least by store politics, he was very professional and a top bloke. I went past Judy's office to go to the loo whilst she was being interviewed by him and she looked very red in the face and extremely uncomfortable.

Whilst the situation was ongoing, I was in dispensary, and I felt that someone was watching me. I looked up and about thirty feet away was a regular customer, who was sadly in the last stages of cancer and was an absolute sweetheart. He beckoned me over and said, "Kim I am not going anywhere near there pointing to the dispensary". I asked him why, and he said that a few weeks ago he was sitting in the dispensary chairs, which were out of view to us, and had heard the awful regular pharmacist talking to me no better than a dog. He told me that he was so disgusted that he had decided to write a letter, and he wanted to give it to my manager. I felt terribly awkward and incredibly touched that with all that he was going through he had taken the time to do such an honourable thing. I told him I was so very grateful, but hastily explained that there was something going on regarding her and the way she was treating me. And sadly, for me to take his letter to the manager when the matter was currently being investigated, it would seem contrived, he understood completely and was an incredibly sweet and very brave man.

During this time most people on the shop floor were very supportive, they had known me for a long time, and knew that I was telling the truth. There were a few who were disgusted by what was happening and told my manager precisely what they thought, which was brave of them. One in particular my pal Sara put her head firmly above the parapet, in more ways than one. She was 15 years younger than me and had more balls than most people I have ever met. I was so grateful to her and brought her a silver bracelet, which was insufficient for all that she did, she was an absolute little star.

The result of my grievance was that the witnesses from the other store were irrelevant because it didn't appertain to them, their grievances were a separate matter. I was praised for my exemplary work record and Pollyanna had admitted to the smallest amount of inappropriate behaviour and was going to apologise to me. This letter was sent to my old marital address, I am certain deliberately as they had all my current contact info on file, no doubt to reduce the five-day appeal period. I expect courtesy of the delightful area manager. I was totally exhausted with no more gladiator style spirit left in me; the song would have had no effect.

Judy was very swiftly transferred to a much smaller branch closer to her home. When we crossed paths in the stores lift foyer just before she left, I politely said to her "Judy you were so wrong about this, one day you will find out that I told the absolute truth". I felt it incredibly strongly but had no clue as to how she would ever be enlightened.

A new manager came to the store, and I told her that I was not coping at all, and I could not be expected to work any longer with Pollyanna. I asked her why the company had not even made her apologise for the small amount of bad behaviour that she had admitted. She was professional and said she would try and get me a transfer to another store, which she did. Luckily the same day a decent manager from a different branch told her that he would be more than happy to have me. Also, I would get to work once more with my old manager/pharmacist who was one of the nicest people on earth, normal services were soon to be resumed.

I transferred stores the following day and within a few weeks I was told that Pollyanna had targeted another healthcare staff member. A young healthcare assistant was off sick and been prescribed anti-depressants. And was refusing to go back into work unless something was done to address Pollyanna's behaviour. Another worker was so upset by something Pollyanna had said to her, she was found crying in the foetal position on the stock room floor.

While Pollyanna was still working at my previous store, she came down several times to conduct an unrequested " welfare check". She made a point of standing near the dispensary as if she was looking for a particular item, she truly was bonkers.

My pharmacist said don't rise to it Kim just ignore her, she is trying to intimidate you, she will stop it in the end, which eventually she did. Something else also happened that was extremely strange and did frighten me. One morning my colleague answered the dispensary phone and said, "It's for you Kim" and passed the phone to me. I said "Hello how can I help?" and then a male voice, whom I didn't recognize began creepily singing my name over and over again, and saying that he was going to get me. Whoever it was sounded like they were completely off their face on drugs, or drink. I was in shock and immediately spoke to my manager, who insisted that when I left work that the store security guard or a male colleague always accompanied me to my car. I had no one with an agenda against me who would ever threaten me; the only person who had any issue with me was Pollyanna who had a new boyfriend. Another pharmacist had previously told me that potentially the pyramid of red bull may have had a link to a certain recreational past time which he had witnessed at a party. I was worried that there may have been a link, and I was going to be attacked in the stores car park and was bricking it for several weeks.

A few of the regular customers had gone into my old store and had asked where I was and very sweetly came down to my new branch to thank me and say goodbye. One who I really liked was called Evelyn she was in her early eighties, razor sharp, very funny and as feisty as they come. She asked me why I had left in such a hurry, and that something must have happened. I thought sod it I will tell her, and I did, she was furious and had been one of the customers that had told me Pollyanna had creeped her out. We had a chat and our usual giggle, and I wished her all the very best for the future and thanked her for making such an effort to visit me.

I didn't expect to see her again but the following week she came back, and gleefully informed me "I went into the store Kim and there was a queue of people at dispensary, and when she eventually came over to serve me, I told her Kim, I bloody told her good and proper that she was a nasty low life bully and while she worked there, I wouldn't get my prescription from her if my life depended on it"

Thank you Evelyn, God Bless you little beauty

Soon after Pollyanna was sent to manage a very small branch in the country. After about a month there and more of the same old behaviour, an extremely astute staff member took the matter into her own hands # big respect. She told her " If this company isn't ever going to do something about you then I am". And she proceeded to threaten to ring the Pharmaceutical Society and report her for bullying. Job finally done; Pollyanna made a very quick exit back to her homeland.

A few years passed and I wondered whether there had been any further "activity" with regards to Pollyanna. I don't know why, but I had a gut feeling that she would have continued this behaviour. And indeed, she had, as soon as she had got off the plane and started a new job, she did precisely the same. In a case that was documented in the media that was related to employment law and was also a very clear case of bullying.

The sad fact is that sensitive, kind and thoughtful people are often targeted by narcissists and psychopaths. We irritate them, and they wrongly assume that we are weak, stupid and sensitive and our empathy is something which can be used against us.

Some like Pollyanna are far worse than others and they should be avoided at all costs, as soon as you know just what you are dealing with run for the hills, but when it is a work colleague it is impossible to do so. If you outwit them, they will immediately react by playing dirty and they will win... why? Because they are consummate actors who have the ability to smarm their way into jobs, people's affections and good books. Often people who you have trusted will be convinced by their star performance. I wish I could say it is possible to get the upper hand with them, but you never will. Because to do so you would have to do the impossible and stoop as low as a snake's belly which would be impossible for anyone with a modicum of decency and self-respect. If you out them they will not learn or self-reflect and will simply move swiftly onto the next target. By walking away, you may feel that you have lost but you have won, and you will eventually recover but they will remain forever trapped in their empty void.

Bullying is abhorrent it destroys children's lives, people commit suicide because of it and days and days are lost in the workplace because of the huge amount of stress it places people under. A perpetrator will always do it to puff themselves up because of an empty void that lies within them. We have all seen photos of some of the most beautiful looking teenagers both male and female, who take themselves away from a world that would benefit so much from their presence all because of spineless, and weak individuals. Bullying whether it is physical, mental or cyber is a disgusting thing to do to another living soul.

Good luck to anyone who is experiencing the same, speak out and be brave, it's only happening to you because something beautiful shines within, keep your light shining bright it is something very special that they can never extinguish.

Song Choice: (Lyrics do not marry up completely with this scenario, but we are all a united band of brothers and sisters and I love this song:)

Diamonds by Rihanna

15 THE STAIRWAY

To Heaven

Our border collie was such a beautiful soul, and my best furry girlfriend. We brought her from a local farm, and she was from working stock. There were ten puppies in the litter who were kept in large barn, all of them looked healthy and incredibly sweet. My eyes were naturally drawn to one who was sitting alone at the back of the group, and of course I wanted to take it home immediately. The puppies at the front of the group were running around and did not remain still for more than a couple of seconds. Baby Girl was slap bang in the middle of the group and was neither worried nor going bat shit mental.

Dad knew precisely how to pick a dog, and she had instantly caught his attention. And said to me "What about this one Kim"? He told me to pick her up and to see if she was comfortable with me. I carefully scooped her up, and she reached up to my face and gave me the biggest wettest kiss, instantly I was a goner. Thirty minutes later she was sitting on dad's lap whilst I drove us all home. It was a miracle that we got home in one piece, as I was not concentrating on the road. I could barely take my eyes off the most beautiful little bundle of black and white fur.

When she was allowed out for her first post vaccination walk my daughter and I took her to a nearby field at the end of the road. Dad had given us strict instructions that she must not be let off the lead. We obeyed for a short period of time, but as she looked so relaxed and was so little, I foolishly removed her lead. I wrongly assumed that as she was so small there was no way she would ever be able to outrun us. Of course, it was a very bad move as she immediately took off like a whippet, with Faye and I in hot pursuit. She soon outran us and much to our dismay we lost sight of her. And conducted a search of the entire area for forty minutes but to no avail, we couldn't find her.

I knew that I would get it all guns blazing when I told dad what had happened, and I deserved everything that was about to come my way. Sheepishly we returned home, and I explained what had happened. It was entirely my fault and there was no point saying otherwise. Dad looked extremely serious for all of five minutes and didn't utter a single word. He walked away and we were absolutely bricking it... and returned five minutes later with her in his arms. Although she had never been out before she had found her way home, and Dad had spotted her sitting by the wheelie bin. Collies are incredibly clever, and I thank God she was, as I would never have forgiven myself if she had been injured or we hadn't found her.

She was his little shadow for sixteen years; and he would sit with her when I had gone to bed, and they would have their lengthy chats. Dad talking in his very deep voice telling her she would always be with him no matter what. Dad struggles with people, but his Princess never judged him, and they were as thick as thieves, think Monty Don and Nigel it was that kind of dynamic.

We had a different but equally special relationship; she was my furry angel and I used to tell her so. I knew that without a shadow of a doubt she like me picked up on any changes in atmosphere and noticed anything spooky at precisely the same time. She loved my dire singing too, now that is the real deal and I used to make up little songs for her. Latterly when I was playing my newly acquired ukulele she would sit on the rug in the conservatory, and she particularly liked Rule the World by Take That.

She had far too many pet names and as she was a super intelligent collie, she responded to them all. These included Baby Girl, Princess Pudding, Bumble, Bumbalina and my dad's very unusual one "the bestest girl in the boy's class".

In her twilight years she had a sensitive tummy and had to eat gastrointestinal friendly food and cooked chicken. Dad was very particular with her food and rightly so, however on the QT she was partial to a Quaver. I used to go into the kitchen and put my finger up to my lips as if to say "shush". That was her signal to come over to me without dad seeing her from the living room. She didn't eat anything on her last day apart from a Quaver, which I gave to her in front of him. There was no need for secrecy at that point.

Dad absolutely adored her and the thought of losing her troubled him greatly. He has always been a dog lover and owner and the loss of his three previous dogs had affected him a great deal. He often spoke about them and although they had all lived long lives and he had spent many happy years with them. The day that each of them had been put to sleep still troubled him tremendously and he would often talk about it. I knew that if his latest doggy loves impending departure to Rainbow Bridge" was conducted with as much love and dignity as possible that it may help him this time in the grieving process.

How we pass over is extremely important, if time permits. It gives us an opportunity to make the process as peaceful as possible for our loved ones, in whatever earthly form they take. I once watched a You Tube programme about the subject. Dr Peter Fenwick was discussing passing over, and what he thinks happens before during and after the process. He is a neuropsychologist and has conducted studies in a few Countries with nurses, family members and patients who knew that they were going to die.

I thought it may be morbid viewing but surprisingly it was an extremely comforting watch. One of his colleagues who had a terminal illness, promised him that if anything that they had discussed or had found in their studies, happened to him he would tell his wife "Tell Peter this has happened". And in the transitional period between life and death he did confirm one phenomenon. Apparently mentally letting go of all that is down here, houses, people possessions etc prior to passing makes it easier and more peaceful. Nurses who witnessed deaths in which the person was calm and at peace said the whole room was often filled with the most beautiful white light just before they departed. Also, birds of all types frequently landed on windowsills during this time which is a lovely thought. He explained why so many people pass when a loved one just leaves the room to "get a cup of coffee or some fresh air". He said it was because the person is still connected physically to their loved one, and so they linger for a little longer. But the time in which they are alone is a window of opportunity for the soul to depart peacefully.

When Baby Girl was thirteen, I decided to take the best photo of her that I could and put it away. So that when she passed over, it would be a lovely reminder of her which had not been on display before. We were very blessed and had her for almost three more years.

However, when she was almost sixteen it was clear that she was naturally winding down and was not going to be around for much longer. It would have been the perfect end if she had passed away naturally, but I knew that more than likely we would have to make the decision for her.

I couldn't bear to think of her in the back of the car wrapped in a towel or an old blanket on her journey to the crematorium. So, one afternoon I made her what I called her "special sleeping bag". I had some beautiful turquoise Sanderson material and proceeded to make a drawstring bag, with a little toy rabbit attached and internal pocket so that I could put a little note in from us both. Once I had completed it, I showed it to her and told her that one day she would be inside it. And then she would go on a magical journey to a place where she could run and hang out with lots of other dogs and eat Quavers whenever she wanted to. Although collies can apparently recognize a thousand words and I know that she did, my story was pushing my luck. But she sat there looking at me with her wise old eyes that mirrored the love we shared.

I also purchased a large crystal that you hang in the window to throw rainbow prisms of light around the room, which I thought would be a direct visual link to Rainbow Bridge, when the time for her journey came.

Two weeks before her journey, she was sitting in her tried and tested poncing spot in the new house, positioned in the doorway between the kitchen and living room. And I decided to have a chat with her, and film it, I sat beside her. And I told her what a beautiful girl she was and that she was my little angel. I thanked her for all the love and unwavering loyalty she had given to us throughout her life and told her just how very special she was, and that she would soon be going to heaven, and she would love it. I described all the funny and energetic things she was going to do, and I promised her that we would meet up again before she knew it.

On the morning of May 10th, we awoke, and her back legs had gone overnight, it was very sudden, but we both knew it had been coming. It was her birthday and sadly to also to be her last. It was the date that my grandmother had passed, and the date that I had decided to look for dad, there was a spot of spiritual synchronicity going on.

We both remained calm throughout the day, I fed her a Quaver, and dad cuddled and talked to her. She couldn't drink from a bowl, so I cupped some water in my hand, she drank a little a few times, and gave me three goodbye kisses. It was a lovely sunny day and we placed her on her bed in the garden. She was with us, in nature and could hear the birds singing.

I was absolutely determined that our little furry mucker would travel to heaven peacefully. We took it in turns sitting quietly with her in the sun over a few hours, hoping that the garden would be the place that she crossed over. However, she held on and as the weather cooled, we brought her back indoors.

In the early evening, I decided to play a few peaceful songs in the background to help us all. I didn't want her to feel our sadness, I wanted her to be calm. As you know by now my music taste is very eclectic, and if I am in my chillout zone, I play Vangelis 1492, Gregorian chants, Enya, Clannad and Hildegard Von Bingen. One song that I think is beautiful and is about passing over, and the transition between earth to heaven is Enyas Evening Falls. This I played a couple of times for her, and she was so still, I willed her to go at this point, but she still clung on.

I gently spoke to her and once more reassured her that she was going to a very special place where she could run around and play with other dogs. Dad listened whilst I asked her if she could do me a big favour. Which was to somehow let me know she had arrived safely in her new home, either by sending me some white feathers, a butterfly or a robin.

She remained peaceful until 10.30 pm that evening, and although we had made an appointment the following day to say our official goodbyes, unfortunately her breathing rate increased. Luckily, we managed to get an emergency appointment, so she didn't suffer for longer than twenty minutes.

We said our goodbyes in the boot of the car, in the veterinary practice's car park due to coronavirus. It was situated in a very peaceful rural location; the night sky was very clear and there was a very calming gentle breeze. It was very private, and the vet and nurse were very kind, and swift in their actions. She fell asleep surrounded by familiar smells, with a big goodbye kiss from both of us. We brought her home wrapped up in the vet's blanket and then put her in her own special bag and laid her in the conservatory. Dad stayed with her until he felt it right to come to bed.

He had arranged a slot to have her cremated in a well-run and caring pet cemetery for the following morning. Before we left, I said a prayer and played her favourite song "Rule the World" on my uke. And placed a note in her sleeping bags pocket, telling her just how very special and loved she was.

I went to make us a cuppa before we left home, and suddenly dad shouted, "Quick Kim look out in the garden". Slowly floating down in front of the conservatory where she lay was the biggest white feather it was beautiful. I stood and looked at Princess and then blow me down another gently fell, she had arrived at Rainbow Bridge safely.

Before we left for the crematorium, we went one last time to her favourite place the beach. Dad drove and parked the car reversing in so that Baby Girl was facing the sea. I remained in the passenger seat, whilst they both had one last look at the sea together. Dad suddenly shouted "Kim get out of the car quick now" I wondered what the hell was going on and did so quick sharp. For a nano second, I thought that a miracle had happened, it had been a "Bobby Ewing" moment, and she wasn't dead after all. He told me to look at the sea, and it was beautiful with white waves over the entire expanse that looked like galloping horses. I asked him what the phenomena was, and he replied, "White Horse waves you don't see them very often". I could not believe that my childhood song had played a part on that very sad day, it was perfect timing and incredibly comforting.

We then took her to the crematorium; I carried her in and laid her on the rimmed table ready for the crematoriums manager to take her through. I said my goodbyes and went outside to wait in the car with dad. On route just outside the crematorium was a beautiful tree lined avenue which had a red rubber ball left on the path. I walked over to it and picked it up and threw it and said "This is for you" just in case she was having a sneaky peak at me from Rainbow Bridge.

Whilst we were waiting for her, I picked some wildflowers from around the car park to place on her casket when we arrived home. The manager of the crematorium was incredibly kind, it was very clear that it was not just a job to him. He did it because he loved animals and completely understood their owner's grief. He walked towards the car with her in a casket within a little brown bag with her name on, and it had a sprig of white flowers attached to it. We thanked him profusely for all he had done for us and left for home.

This time she was on my lap whilst dad drove, and I held her close to me. It was a very physical reminder of life and death. Our earthly journey together was complete, but I know we will see her again one day.

When we arrived home, I placed her casket and the flowers on the sideboard. And I went to my bedroom to get the photo which I had taken three years previously. Dad had not seen it and loved it, and I hung it on the wall behind the telly. Whilst doing so I noticed that on her left shoulder, there was a small patch of rainbow reflected light. When I had taken the photo there was nothing nearby that could have caused a prism of light. The crystal that I had hung in the window a few weeks prior to her death threw many beautiful rainbow lights around the room and made me feel that I was connected to the rainbow. Rainbows end that I could see but would not be able to reach until my time was up. The film that I shot also gave dad and I a great deal of comfort.

After our last beach outing, I began trawling Ebay for a permanent reminder of the day. I entered in White Horses and found the most beautiful retro framed print. The colours were beautiful, a turquoise base and the horses looked so strong and almost magical. I wanted to secure it. It was not available to buy now, with no submit an offer its starting price was £35. I contacted the seller and told him truthfully why I wished to purchase the print but I did not mention the song. I offered him £75, and much to my delight he accepted my offer and said he would alter the listing, so that I could buy it straight away. From that point onwards everything went pear shaped. It flashed up that I could buy it now, then this option disappeared when I confirmed payment, and nothing was showing up his end although he had done all that he should. We thought that a third party was interfering with one or both of our Ebay accounts. I told him that I would bid for it and hopefully would win, and he wished me all the luck in the world. I bid for the item and won it for a fiver less than I had offered. I was made up and promptly performed one of my arthritic victory dances.

About three days later it arrived and the amount of care he had taken to ensure it arrived safely was incredibly thoughtful. Also, there was a very carefully cut out paper chameleon on the top left-hand side of the packaging, where a stamp would normally be positioned. I knew that it had been purposely placed there, and so I carefully removed it and looked up its meaning which is: "The chameleon has a shining personality, always displaying courage and boldness with every human contact, the chameleon symbolism teaches a lot about fearlessness and curiosity and knowing when to cloak yourself into the background." I sent an email thanking him for the extra care he had taken wrapping the print and for the chameleon stamp. He replied that it had been a joint endeavour and that he and his partner had packaged the item, and he was so pleased that it had arrived safely. I sent my final thanks to him and told them the extra personal bit of information about the song "White Horses" by Jacky. A short while later an email came through saying what a beautiful sunny day it had been and he and his partner had been sitting in their garden with a bottle of wine, and they had played the song and had raised their glasses and made a toast to Baby Girl and such a perfect day.

I know that this may sound a little OTT if you are not an animal person, but I expect many of you do the same or far more than we did. The loyalty and love these beautiful souls give often surpasses anything that human beings are willing or able to impart to their fellow man. I have always found this a little sad that a silent sentient little soul, covered in fur can comfort another species without one word ever needing to be spoken, they truly are incredibly special.

Although the grieving process must run its natural course and cannot be reduced or lessened. The things I did prior to and on the day, itself did help dad. When he looks back on the day that she passed, he will say " I still miss her, but we did her proud and could have done no more".

Song: Whistle My Love by Elton Hayes

Dedicated to Princess Pudding, and our Little Pickle who are up on Rainbow Bridge and also to the wonderful Paul O'Grady. Although I didn't know him, like millions of others I felt that I did. A very special soul who is of course up there too partying with his human buddy's in-between being chief dog whisperer and head walker.

Thank you, Paul, from all your fellow animal lovers down here, it's official

you were the mutts's nuts. X

Song: You've Got a Friend by James Taylor

ROOM 16

The Advocate

The world has always been unfair and for a reason that was completely unrelated to my childhood, I knew from the earliest of ages that many people were not treated equally. And I felt it was my duty to highlight inequality and favouritism whenever I witnessed it. The word unfair was often on the tip of my tongue, and it will remain there and be ready to be spoken if needed, until I die.

As an introvert I feel far more comfortable highlighting injustices by using the written word, and spotting discrepancies to deconstruct arguments. Which has been used to discredit a person or to push an unfair outcome. As well as standing up for myself, I have done this for friends and work colleagues who have wanted to purvey that they have taken legal advice. Writing a personal account of my life has been difficult and does not come naturally to me. I love trawling through pages of information and finding that one salient point that others may have missed, to highlight and address an unfair situation.

I am the invisible fixer, the person who in a group observes everything from the back of the room. And often from under my INFJ invisibility cloak, I will quietly say a valid point which is then adopted by someone else as their own. This doesn't bother me as I am far happier being well under the radar and allows me to see the whole picture, I take in far more information by not being in the mix. I struggle with small talk, and I am always searching for meaningful communication on how we can improve ourselves and the world that we live in. INFJ'S are often ahead of the curve and can see potential problems way before they happen. This is because we see the entire picture and look for patterns and probable outcomes which are based on facts both from past and the present. We then introduce the human element into the equation and how an individual or a group of people are currently thinking. This ability to predict an outcome often leads others to say we are psychic. But how we analyse information which may seem abstract to others is just how our brains process external data, there is nothing remotely woo woo about it.

Here are a few simplistic examples as to how I think and process information as an INFJ, which will be a pre-curser to the next chapter which refers to intuition-based thinking which relates to abstract patterns and frequency of events. And the following chapter, which is dedicated to unexplainable phenomena, which is juxtaposed to how I process information. So, when you reach a conclusion about an upcoming and particularly "out there" event which I experienced, I hope by way of a defence you could take the following into the equation...

Logic Based & Observational Thinking

In my workplace bullying chapter I mentioned an incident that I had reported to the police and my suspicions had been correct.

One afternoon we were short staffed, and I was running between the dispensary and the healthcare counter. Towards the end of the day a female customer came in and asked for hydrogen peroxide, which can be used for a number of reasons when diluted. I proceeded to retrieve the item from the drawer, and then she asked me whether we sold baking powder. Immediately I knew the combination was used to make improvised bombs. So, whilst I was explaining to her that we didn't sell it, I began logging everything that I possibly could about her appearance, so I could report the incident to the police when I got home. I would rather have been wrong and made myself look foolish than for anyone to lose their life in a terror attack. An officer from the terrorist branch came to interview me the following day and the companies investigational officer aided him with regards to CCTV. After this the sale of hydrogen peroxide was no longer permitted throughout the company's branches.

I was told a couple of years later by the companies investigating officer that the same female had gone into several chemists in the area with the same request, and I had been correct in my deduction.

For a few years I was a Special Constable and during one training session, our observational skills were assessed. The sergeant showed us a video of a robbery at a local petrol station, in real time, and we individually had to recall what we had seen. I watched intently and was happy with how much information I had gleaned from the five-minute clip. And then much to my dismay gradually each person in the group when recalling what they had seen had slightly differing accounts. I was the last person in a group of fifteen to be asked my take on the robbery, and I felt sick at the prospect of being laughed at. For a moment I wondered whether it would be best to change my account to one that fitted the room dynamic, and then I would remain under the radar and be able to save some face. But I decided not to, if I made myself look like an idiot, it would be a lesson learned, and I would pay more attention in the future. And so, I proceeded to relay my altered state of reality version, and of course a couple of new recruits jokingly took the proverbial and asked me whether I had been on the same planet and had I smoked a spliff before buying my petrol! I took it in good part and then when the friendly banter stopped. The sergeant said that he had news for the group, I hadn't been on the wacky baccy, and I was the most sober in the group. I had logged all of the salient information that was available to give a bang on witness statement.

<u>Intuition</u>

Evidence gathering that is factually based does enable us to often have the heads up prior to others. But to confirm our immediate take on a situation we also draw on our intuition. INFJ's are normally in a state of reflection and quiet introspection and tend not to take things solely on face value and look beyond what is initially presented to us or what we are told.

Recently our elderly rescue dog became incredibly weak, detached and confused overnight. And when he cocked his leg to have a wee, he squatted down like a stallion. Logic linked these three facts, and I came to the conclusion that there could be something wrong with his urinary tract, and he possibly had an infection. We made and emergency appointment and saw a vet who thoroughly checked the little fellas' heart, temperature and breathing rate. However, he was very focused on how weak and detached he was and also his age. He explained that if there was no improvement by 4.45 pm that afternoon it would be the kindest course of action to put him to sleep. Dad was extremely upset but fully on board with what the vet had advised. But I acted on my intuition and put it to the vet that I felt he could possibly have an infection relating to the urinary tract. I asked whether he would consider the possibility and give him the highest dose permitted of a broad-spectrum antibiotic in the form of an injection. My reasoning being was that if he was dying it would not be in the least bit detrimental, and it may give him a chance. He didn't agree but because I was upset and wouldn't drop it, he reluctantly agreed and gave him an injection. With a heavy heart we were told to make a provisional appointment seven hours later to ensure that he was not suffering, which reluctantly we did. Initially there was no improvement and he remained very weak and was well away with the fairies. But over the following three hours he gradually became aware of his surroundings and was far brighter. I cancelled the euthanasia appointment, but asked to keep the slot so that he could be checked once more.

The vet was surprised by the clear improvement and decided to check his prostrate, which was very enlarged and more than likely infected. Just as an elderly human could become disorientated and confused with an UTI the same had happened to our elderly dog. The vet was a little embarrassed and contrite that he had made a wrong assessment. I told him that it truly didn't matter, and I was just incredibly grateful that he had given in to my protestations. He prescribed antibiotics for five weeks, and our little boy made a complete recovery. A perfect example of evidence gathering and an INFJ's intuition at work...

All very logical and evidence-based thought processes, but some things do defy logic. And just as most human beings are somewhat paradoxical the world in all of its glory is too.

Check out a brilliant husband and wife duo on YouTube called The Hound & The Fox.

Song: The Paradox

THE HALL OF MIRRORS 17

All An Illusion?

We all interpret song lyrics differently and as a child I loved the song Strawberry Fields which is admittedly a little odd. For me it represented living in an altered state of reality, one in which you were pretending that all was ok when it wasn't, and everything was in fact and an illusion. We are all currently living in such as state, and we have been for many years now, and sadly it is getting worse. There is a blurring of reality between what is real and what is fake, what is deemed normal and what is not.

A great deal of the worlds current advertising seems to be far too colourful, garish, cartoonish and out and out weird. It is de-humanizing mankind and trying to remove the human element behind our thoughts which effects our decision-making abilities.

When I see The Lloyds Black Horse advert, which I know is a computer-generated image. I feel relief that my brain is not having to register and decipher what the advert represents and means. I also love the Rolex advert as it shows humanity, and depicts our strengths and weaknesses, whoever wrote it was bang on point. But in the main most adverts do not relate remotely to the product, and if they do a ten-year-old could have cobbled together the narrative. For example, the Lenor

Outdoorable advert "Where is the Sun?" Presumably the intended target market is five-year-olds who do the family shop. And someone actually got paid a shed load of money to come up with that masterpiece. If that was made to appeal to the mass market and they think we truly relate to such puerile drivel, we really are up the proverbial without a paddle.

Children are being encouraged to buy energy drinks such as Prime which exceed the normal recommended intake of caffeine for an adult. And then we are wondering why our children are suffering from mental health issues and are stressed to the absolute max. In between begging their parents to buy every different flavour and coloured bottle of this toxic product, they watch adverts which ridicule the beauty of this earth. I was incredulous when I saw an advert for a new gaming device which was shot on the top of one of the most beautiful mountains, which of course was completely irrelevant and of secondary importance. As the player sat on a rock engrossed in the red piece of plastic in his hand.

I love YouTube it is the one app which I do use on my smartphone. But if I ever look at it when I am not logged in, the first page that comes up is awash with weird and overly colourful images, ideas and latest trends. I haven't got a clue who Mr Beast is, but his overly exaggerated smile and features looks like an animated version of a human being. It is incredibly creepy, and children are looking at this as if it is the norm, when it is the reverse. I feel it is done to dehumanize mankind and to turn as many of us as possible into a walking talking smartphone, which reacts to images rather than human contact. Without a shadow of a doubt, it is working as many people are not remotely connected with their actual surroundings, their children or pets. They walk around detached and completely in their own personal technology driven bubble.

Recently a few popstars seem to have completely lost the plot. And they believe that the only way they can remain current and relevant, is to crank the weird up to the absolute max. Madonna has always been out to shock and there is nothing wrong with that to a degree, but she has taken things too far. And quite frankly her appearance and her general demeanour is disturbing. During one recent interview she was crawling around suggestively and was very animalistic. To be honest if she had begun scuttling around like a possessed crab, it wouldn't have surprised me in the least. I still love some of her music particularly Frozen and Live to Tell, it is awful what fame does to some people. A very talented lady who has completely lost the plot and there are many more like her coming up through the ranks.

Such as Sam Smith who has a beautiful voice, and who seemed such a lovely chap when he first came onto the music scene. He probably is still a nice bloke but is just making ill informed decisions. The terribly disturbing video of him parading around half naked and looking not dissimilar to Herod in the Passion of the Christ, was not a good look for many different reasons. And also emulating "He who must not be named" is a very bad move. He may have thought it was all harmless fun, just as Madonna did when she had a photo shoot which depicted that she had attended The Last Supper. Anyone who does similar may think it is the ultimate shock factor, and for a few earthly minutes yes indeed it is. But I am without doubt that when their mortal time on earth is up, fame, money and ego's will not come into the equation when they are given a choice that will last for eternity.

And as for the Paris Olympic Games opening ceremony doing the same it went beyond the pale. I strongly suspect that The European Union had a great deal of input with this narrative and the clear message that was being sent out to the world. Blasphemy and the book of Revelation re-enacted courtesy of Europe's equivalent to the House of Babel. Just what an innocent child wants to see, I thought the Singing Ringing Tree was as bad as it could get, but they managed to top it.

Anything that is too loud, too colourful, too unusual and out right weird like this avoid looking at it. Make your own definition and set your own clear boundaries not just for yourself but for your loved ones, particularly if they are impressionable or vulnerable. Our world is becoming so surreal and it is dumbing down mankind's intellect, as well as taking away our capacity to communicate with one and other. We spend most of our lives hooked up to equipment that knows precisely where you are, and what we are doing and what your likes and dislikes are. Even when you take photos on your phone, it will set you up a lovely little collage of your photos, a collage that you have not constructed or requested. And when you wake up in the morning and start moving about your phone suddenly starts sending you notifications, because it has a microphone and sensor that hears and feels your movements.

Technology is currently out of control and it is getting far worse. I believe that in the future, it will be so advanced that it will be able to generate an image that will convince a very large amount of people to believe what they are seeing without questioning it, and they will blindly follow its lead. A road that should never be trodden, and one that will take us further down the proverbial shitter than we already are.

Because our brains operate to be essentially logical, we think that computers input has come from a man that it cannot be interfered with by anything other than man. Which is wrong although men can interfere with programmes, hack them and cause havoc. Also bad energy can do the same, it sounds crazy but I know it is absolutely true. Which is precisely why we must keep using cash that cannot be influenced by anything other than ourselves. Often there is a queue at the self service cash and card tills, because something has "gone down" and there is only one cash till available. In the queue most of us say the same "They are trying to make it as awkward as possible" so we become a cashless society" it is so blinking obvious. And no thank you Mr Gates I do not want a microchip inserted anywhere with a patent no with 060606 in the mix!

The most vulnerable and open to suggestion will be those who are addicted to their smartphones and have been induced into an almost zombie like catatonic state. Those who are still lucid and function autonomously will question the majorities perception and will be proven right after a long battle of wills. A battle that I hope does not happen in my lifetime, but if it does like millions of others, I will stand my ground.

Just as I know that there is a beautiful and peaceful thin area between heaven and earth. Sadly, there is another area which is regularly visited and used by various groups. I am in no doubt that this area can often portray information, which is accurate and seemingly good, but essentially the source behind it is not always pure.

I have seen and experienced phenomena from that area in the form of a ghost and I have also seen items being moved, and there is absolutely no rational explanation. Because I am very logical it unnerved and confused me, which is of course why I was shown it. The area works in many different ways and can invoke fear and confusion, as it did for me. But also, it can intrigue and entice by pretending to come from a good source. It works by deception and trickery, and it is an unsettling and heavy area which although real it is based on illusion. It should not be entertained, encouraged, played with and most importantly it should never be believed. If you see anything or hear anything that frightens you completely ignore it, deny its existence don't play into it and pray to God.

As I often look at religious sites on YouTube which I trust both for guidance and prayers. Occasionally I will pass a message on to others if I feel it necessary to do so. I have told a few people about this story when they have told me that they have been to see a medium or such like.

Sadly, as it was a one-off viewing, I cannot remember this dear souls name, so I will call her Sister Terese. Who is a nun from France. and as well as spreading Gods word for many years in the usual way, she also has a YouTube channel to reach out to the wider world. I am sure she will forgive me for not relaying her story verbatim, but this is the gist of it. Her childhood was extremely happy, and she was nestled within a family who had a very strong Catholic faith. All was well until she was in her twenties, when she felt that she needed to see the wider world and travel, and so she did. One place that always intrigued her was India and she stayed there for a while. One day she visited a village with a companion who was familiar with the area. And a man came out from one of the huts and began talking to her. He invited her into his home to get out of the sun and to have a drink of water with him. To which she agreed, and they chatted for a while, during which he told her that he had a gift for her. He went into the back room and returned with a book, and she asked him what it was. He told her that it was her life story, and she doubted the validity of his words. She had never met him before and how would he have been able to write in her native tongue. She opened the book and to her amazement he had, it was her life story, all of it right up until that point. Things he could never have known about her, she was shocked, and felt unsettled but thanked him and left.

From that moment onwards she gradually lost her true essence and felt uncertain about her life's path. Before it was always connected entirely to God, she was strong and at peace, and now she was not. She became depressed, uncertain and confused about her life and where it was heading. What if he knew her future. What if it was mapped out and was not what she wanted? She would do the bare minimum and spend many hours at home feeling isolated and alone. She stopped going to church and at times felt suicidal. Her sister who lived close by was incredibly worried about her, but Terese would rarely listen when she raised her concerns. However, one day she told her that she must come back to church because she was worried about the dramatic change in her personality. And that she loved her dearly and if she did not attend the next service, she felt that she would not be on this earth much longer. And so, Terese went with her sister as she had done many times before. But this time she felt odd and disconnected, her beloved church no longer felt like her home. The service continued and suddenly she began to cry and scream. The congregation were afraid but also worried about her, they all prayed for her whilst she was shouting and screaming until she eventually stopped. Immediately she no longer felt disconnected with her forever home and shed many tears. Terese knew then her calling was to be a nun and to tell people her story...

And now it is time for my confession, as well as having the deepest regret that I did not read the bible sooner, there was a ramification for not doing so, and one that I repent daily for. I owned items that I thought were ok and they were not. Although I have always believed in God, I confess that I have had crystals in my home, a dream catcher, and buddhas because they have peaceful expressions, and my mum once brought me a pack of guardian angel cards. All seemingly innocuous items, and as I had always prayed and believed in God, and worshipped only him what harm could they possibly be? Looking back with the benefit of hindsight I was on an arse covering mission. Life was not always easy and I was trying to cover every base. A little bit of protection here and there in conjunction with my faith was surely going to keep me safe from all of life's little nasties. But as soon as I read the bible, I realized that these items have no place in a true Christians life. I had made a very serious error of judgement and in affect I had my feet placed in two camps. And so, I got rid of everything remotely New Age in my home and I repented. That repentance is ongoing and just because I have said sorry once it does not cut the mustard, and I still ask God for his forgiveness about my New Age items. Although I would consider myself to be essentially a good soul, as soon as I binned these items, I felt much lighter and cleaner in spirit and far more connected and closer to God. These items are extremely harmful, and I would implore anyone who truly believes in God not to spiritually arse cover. You will be absolutely fine, bin the items and don't pass them onto anyone else.

The light, the truth and God are all that we should believe in and follow. So, let's head on out to the next room and get the designers in to sort this one out. I'm thinking a white, light, simple and airy theme to compliment the next room, there is nothing like a spot of symmetry:)

Song: Land of Confusion by Genesis

THE SECRET GARDEN 18

The Wonderful

And now onto the area between the two realms: earth and heaven. A place which is beautiful wonderous and pure. A very personal and private area in which God makes you aware of his love for you by showing you signs that cannot be misinterpreted. Signs that are often very simple, spontaneous and often very fleeting but very personal. They are immediately understood and make you feel connected, lighter in spirit, reassured, peaceful and still, or overflowing with gratitude and love.

When I was a baby, my grandfather picked me up from the Children's home and drove many miles from Suffolk to Glastonbury. On arrival, he parked his Ford Anglia at the bottom of the Tor and asked gran to stay in the car and wait for his return. He scooped me up into his arms and strode off up the hill with a great sense of purpose. Gran waited patiently in the car and when he eventually returned, she asked him what an earth had he been doing up there for so long. He told her that he felt I was such a dear little soul that I needed to be protected. He had prayed at the top of the Tor and held me aloft and asked God to always keep me safe for as long as I lived. Not long after I was also baptised COE and I feel incredibly lucky to have been essentially blessed twice.

In all of the properties he lived in Grandad had a buddleia bush, he loved butterflies particularly Red Admirals. At his funeral I was standing to grans left and looked up at a stained-glass window and on the wall next to the window was a Red Admiral. I nudged her and pointed up to the butterfly and we exchanged a knowing smile. We both felt blessed and honoured that we were the only ones to notice it. His funeral was at the beginning of February, and it seemed a little early for one to be alive at that time.

After he had passed away and I had found my natural father, I wanted to go to the RAF base where he had been stationed and had always spoken so fondly of, St Eval in Cornwall. I felt incredibly peaceful on arrival and particularly in the church. I imagined him and all of the brave air men praying before a sortie.

Whilst inside the church I wrote in the church's visitors' book. I proudly wrote his name and the squadron that he had belonged to. And acknowledged the bravery and courage he had displayed for his Country. I then sat on a pew and prayed for peace followed by a simple prayer. When I had spent what I felt was a right amount of time in reflection and prayer I walked outside to meet dad who was waiting in the car for me. As I approached him suddenly a Red Admiral butterfly landed onto my forearm. And I felt immediately that grandad had approved of my visit. I was mesmerized by the butterfly and blow me down several more arrived. I was surrounded by at least eight Red Admirals. Dad was shocked and said, "Kim I don't understand all the stuff you believe in, but I honestly have never seen anything like this before, it looks unreal ".

I have very lucid dreams some of which are incredibly vivid, and they feel as if they are in real time. One such dream was beautiful and comforting but a little bittersweet. Whilst gran was in hospital, and it was inevitable that she was going to pass over very shortly. I went to bed and dreamt that I was standing outside her private room in the middle of the night. I looked towards her bed and the window behind where she slept. It was a very dark clear sky with a few stars which were shining brightly.

The lights were on in the corridor, and it was deadly quiet. Suddenly grandad appeared next to me and said, "Hello My Mishka". He looked much younger and was wearing his RAF uniform. I was so excited to see him again and we hugged one and other. He told me that he wanted to show me something that not many people were allowed to see. And he went on to explain that because I was a spiritual soul, I could watch one part of something very special. But I had to stay precisely where I was, and I must promise not to follow him into the room, to which I agreed.

He told me that he loved me very much and said goodbye and then walked into the room. He sat down on her bed, and his legs in his RAF trousers looked a little too long to be comfortably positioned (his nickname was Lofty in the RAF). He then kissed his wife on her forehead and began to pull her closer to him. A white light filled the room and they both disappeared. I awoke and said to Seb," grans gone now but she is ok". Around fifteen minutes later the hospital rang to tell me that when a nurse had gone in to check on her, she had passed over.

As you know I do believe that in many cases are earthly lives have been mapped out for us for various reasons. All of which are related to spiritual progression and to prepare us for when we leave this mortal coil. Sometimes we can be made aware of the fact that we actually have no control of our destiny, what will be will be.

When I was pregnant with Faye, Seb and my mother and father-in-law decided to book a coach holiday many miles from where we lived. On one excursion we drove down a small road which had a signpost directing you to the local station, and one of the lines destinations which was twenty miles away. Seemingly of no interest, but for many years I would dream of driving down that road and looking at the sign, it had no relevance or so I thought...

I live there now and often walk down that road and past that very sign. I love the place and I know it will be my forever home and I often thank God that I live in what I consider to be the perfect spot for me.

I know that many people see and receive signs that are so beautiful they cannot be anything, but heaven sent. But as you know little Miss Logic here:) struggles with things like that, and subsequently my signs reflect my personality. They usually appear in the form of a tangible object; a songs video will hit the mark or I will bump into just the very person who will show me the way or tell me what I need to hear. I cannot dismiss either as tricks of the light or my imagination, God will find a way to guide you that you will understand and is right for you.

I have had many signs sent to me throughout my life, but over the past few years they have become far more concentrated. Because my occupation involved checking, researching and cross referencing, any unusual item that comes my way I will always check what it means if there is not a clear and obvious connection.

These are a few that have sprung up over the past few years whilst I was working on this book.

Whilst I was out walking in the woods, I was praying and feeling a little perplexed as to why I had been chosen to push a book out into a world that did not want to listen. I was full of self-doubt and although I had not as yet fulfilled my task, I was experiencing imposter syndrome. As I was walking and wondering what an earth was going on, something caught my attention, on the ground in front of me was a little resin heart with tiny flowers within it.

Not long after on another boot sale recce I found some very unusual vintage coasters which I thought were very stylish. They were a very simple design; black with a gold border and a single gold triangle in the centre. I wondered whether a triangle had any significance in the bible and did my usual cross reference... And an equilateral triangle is the symbol of the Holy Trinity.

At another boot sale on a stall was a hand carved wooden bear, sitting on a sleigh, waving and holding the reigns with its other paw. The sleigh was being pulled by three horses and it was very finely carved. I asked the stall holder how much it was and he told me that he wanted a tenner for it because it was so beautifully carved. Because of the bear connection and the horses, it was a no brainer I had to have it. But I was wondering whether I could afford it. And then he piped up "It's Russian you know, and the sleigh is called a Troika". I was nearly there and it felt like yet another sign and then he said it again "It is Russian, the little bear is sitting on a Troika". That was the clincher I brought it, and when I got home, I put a little flag in its waving paw with a heart sticker emblazoned on it.

In the area I was born and raised there was a local printing company which is many miles from where I currently live and although books of course will turn up at boot sales. I found a book printed by the company about "Strong Women" and then one called "Happiness". And a beautiful cube puzzle which has stained glass images on it which you can rearrange that show many different pictures of Saints and angels.

Another boot sale find was an original watercolour painting of a cross that is covered in roses with a single butterfly on it. It was painted by an American artist called Ken Sheldon who works for Hallmark cards. I just love it and my best friend actually recreated a similar cross with flowers for a church service with her schools pupils'. They all went up to a cross that she had constructed out of oasis and they all placed a flower in it until it was full and came to life. Suffice to say I have told her that when I kark it she must have it.

About two months ago I was in my outdoor church on the beach. And I was dismayed at what happening around the world. Such as the increase in random attacks on people just walking in a Country that used to be reasonably safe, and all of the many other atrocities that were increasing. It was getting worse and I know that it is nowhere near as bad as it will get. It was windy, dull and raining and I was already soaked, and my jeans were sticking to my legs. No one was on the beach but me and I dropped to me knees at the shoreline and prayed for things to get better. And then I did something I felt like doing I said Psalm 23 as a plural as in The Lord is our Shepherd we shall not want. I eventually stood up after doing the ungainly roll over and push up move. And I looked towards the area I was heading and about 50ft in front of me was my "Bobbing Balloon" in the form of a buoy. I have been on the beach hundreds of times and I have not seen a single buoy ever wash up there. I went over to it and picked it up and written on it was my Special Constable number. When I got home, I wrote "I believe in Angels" on it and it now hangs up in my nautical themed kitchen.

At the start of this book one of the songs I asked you to play was a particular version of Greensleeves because the graphics are beautiful and go perfectly with the music. All of the graphics are photographic stills which merge into one another. Apart from the final image which is of a watercolour sunset, I planned to replicate the picture and although I am not very good, I do occasionally paint the odd water colour. I also play the song on my ukulele along with other very random songs that are not too difficult. And it appeared at one of the most recent boot sales I attended. On the first stall was an almost replica of this painting in oils, but in a tone that would suit my living room. I brought it for a £5 even though the stall holder had asked for £3.

On the newest version of the video My Sweet Lord it starts off with the groups FBI members searching for what is "out there" in a library. In which two girls are playing cat's cradle which was something I often used to play with my best friend Julia. And finally in the cinema the crazy dude is jumping off the leather armchair and acting the fool just as I did with my daughter when we did our Flashdance routine, and I still do this. Only little things and of course the video has nothing to do with me but it strongly resonated with me.

God and his angels will sometimes give you a boost, and it is often when you are in a very good place. One which is related to gratitude and giving to others selflessly for no reason other than you want to. The smallest of things can make the biggest of differences, regardless of whether I am having a bad day these are things I always do if I can. If you are in a shop and the cashier or shop assistant looks sad or tired, make them feel valued by speaking to them as you would do a friend. Don't be greedy at boot sales it is a pet hate of mine, watching known dealers try and have people over. If you have got a bargain, give them a little more than they have asked for, people really appreciate an act that costs so little. If you do a boot sale and someone genuinely looks on their uppers and they like something that is on your table sell it for a nominal price or give them a freebie, remember one day that person could be you. Always speak to an elderly person who is on their own when you are out and about or simply just smile at them. It won't be long until you are in precisely the same position and would you want to be ignored? A while ago when there was absolutely nothing on television that I liked. I crocheted about thirty small positive potatoes, and always put a few in my pocket or bag when I went out. When I saw someone, I knew whether a shop worker, a friend or a neighbour I gave them one. Every recipient was over the moon and treasure their positive little spuds. I believe that what you put out into the world, if it is done for the right reasons, it will be recognized by God, he knows when you have done his bidding with a true heart. And sometimes he is so pleased with you he will let you know by tipping you the wink, in whatever way he wants to, with his angel helpers at hand.

Not so long ago I wanted to make my mark on the conservatory. Most of the house is very subtly decorated, but I wanted to have a splash of colour in there. I had a fuchsia pink tub chair and a fuchsia pink canvas which had The Dash poem on and I needed a few more items to complete the look. And as a charity shop and boot sale queen off I went to the local boot sale for my usual recce.

The weather was not great and there were only about eight sellers, and I didn't expect to find anything. But much to my delight I found a fuchsia globe light, and two vintage Avon perfume bottles, one a glass butterfly and the other which was white milk glass with a clock face on set at 9.27, the perfumes name was a Moment in Heaven. I also brought a brand-new heater for a fiver all items for the grand some of £11, it was a very lucky day.

Although the house I live in is modern it is important to me that I have a few religious items around me that reflect my faith. Material items mean absolutely nothing to me, but I have a few special items that I would never part with. I purchased from a charity shop a beautiful black and white original photo which has been enlarged and is 20"x 16". It is of the inside of a church and the light is shining through the stained-glass window. The rays of light extend directly onto the church's altar and nowhere else, so it looks like a spotlight is on it. The photographer wrote on the back of it "Let There Be Light". I have it on the wall opposite my bed and around it I have attached some tiny white fairy lights.

I love roses and I have the most beautiful white rose bush in my garden. I know this sounds a little crazy, and all a bit King Charles, but I kiss its leaves seven times once a day when it is starting to come into bud. Last year one branch had the grand total of thirteen beautiful roses on it and it looked just like a large bouquet.

Poem: The Dash by Linda Ellis

Song: I Wonder as I Wander by Simon Khorolskiy

ROOM 19

The Hong Kong Phooey Dilemma

When I was in my late twenties my aunt decided to look for my natural father and asked me whether I was okay with her doing so. I found her request a little odd, because it was not her place to instigate something that would affect me more than anyone else. I suspected that she and mum had decided to have a look for him, and had felt duty bound to tell me, and as I doubted that she would be successful I agreed.

She went to St Catherines House in London and found his marriage certificate, along with a birth certificate relating to his marriage which confirmed a boy had been born a few months prior to my arrival, and then she had drawn a blank. However, the small about of information she had found was very useful and for this I am grateful.

Fast forward ten years and my grandparents had passed over three years previously. Occasionally I thought about the conversation I had with grandad, when he had told me to look for him. One evening I had watched a programme about adult children who had found a natural parent, which gave details of a site that helped people in the same situation which I wrote down. I decided that it would be my one and only attempt to look for him and if I was not successful, I would accept it, safe in the knowledge that I had carried out my grandfather's wishes. The following evening, I went onto the site and entered some information. I listed his name and those who I knew were connected to him along with a polite request as to whether anyone knew where he lived.

I went on my computer the following morning and noticed that there was an email in my inbox, which was a rarity. I opened it and literally overnight I had found him. It was the oddest of feelings; disbelief, excitement and fear all rolled into one. A lady who had been in the same position had found her real father it had turned out well for her and had decided to return the karmic favour. She was in possession of an electoral roll disc, and was able to search for people's names, and had found a clear match. I was so grateful and thanked her profusely, but words did not feel sufficient.

I knew that dad was aware of my existence, so it was a little easier I expect than a child contacting a person who has no clue that they have fathered a child. I decided to write him a letter and was extremely careful as to how I constructed it. I explained who I was, timescales, my mother's name and a little about me. I made it clear that I understood that if he did not want any contact, I would be fine and I meant it. I explained also that I did not resemble any family member and if he could see it in his heart to send me a photo to see if we had any similarities, I would be incredibly grateful. I told him that regardless of what he decided to do I wished him and his family all the very best for the future.

Three days later I was delighted and a little surprised to receive a response from him along with a recent photo. It was a brief but friendly letter and within its contents he told me that he had taught martial arts for many years. Which was at the same time as when I was frantically jumping around my bedroom Hong Kong Phooey style, this I found very poignant. In the letter he also said "I believe there is no such thing as good or bad life, just life" which I thought was very true.

And so, I wrote back to him with a little more information about me and added my phone number under my address. A few days later whilst I was watching DIY SOS my daughter answered the phone and called out "mum there is a strange man on the phone". I took the call expecting it to be a cold caller and was ready to politely decline whatever service was on offer. And much to my surprise it was dad, that moment felt incredibly surreal. He barely drew a breath, and did not once did he ask about me, but I put it down to nerves. However, listening to his voice made him very real to me, he was no longer a dream, and very much a reality.

At the end of the call, we had arranged to meet up two weeks later at my local train station's car park. Several people from work offered to come too and watch at a distance and rescue me if he upset me or was a weirdo. They were an extremely sweet bunch of people and incredibly supportive. But I wanted to go alone so that I could gather my thoughts and be as natural and calm as possible. However, on the actual day my composure had all but deserted me. I was excited but absolutely petrified, my heart was pounding, my mouth was dry, and my hands were absolutely freezing. I scanned my surroundings for his car and spotted him immediately, he smiled and waved, and I walked over in almost a dream like state. I shed a few tears, but I managed to hold it together. The emotion I felt above any at the time was one of the greatest relief, whatever happened and even if I saw him just the once my jigsaw was finally complete.

We chatted for a couple of hours, whilst he drove around the area that I lived, and I asked him all the usual things that you would expect in this situation. He confirmed that he had been very careless as a young man and explained that when he came with mum to see her parents, he did not know what to do. He told me that he was not in love with either of the women whom he had got pregnant and seemed to negate any responsibility for his actions. This annoyed me a little and I pointed out that if he had been careful and responsible then the situation would not have arisen.

When he had visited my grandparents, he felt they were very decent people, who were in a far better position financially to cope with a baby. I listened whilst he explained and the only question, I felt that I needed an answer to; was whether he had ever thought about me when I was a small child. To be honest I doubted that he had because he sounded very immature and reckless. He told me that he had and hoped that I was ok. He was very open and frank throughout our conversation, at times I thought a little too much so, but I was happy that he felt he could trust me. He told me that he had seen a counsellor in the past, as he had been actively planning suicide and also because of a road rage incident. He made light of this, and I presumed that the counselling he had received had been successful and he was now in a far better head space.

At one point we stopped at a garage as he needed some petrol, and before he went to pay, he asked me whether "I would like some sweets"? To which I responded, "It's a bit late for the blinking sweets ". A classic "Kim" one liner which luckily, he found as funny as I did. The time passed quickly, and we chatted away with little awkwardness, which was very surprising under the circumstances, as I am normally guarded when I first meet someone.

He took me home and met Seb and Faye and although it was a little stressful as it was an unusual situation it went well. With the benefit of hindsight, I would say to anyone who is looking for or thinking about locating a natural parent it will not only affect you but all family members on both sides and for this I am sorry.

My roots were shaken, and my entire world seemed to change overnight. I realised that I had to be true to myself and others, I had opinions that were completely different to my remaining family of origin, and without my grandparents I felt alienated and an outsider. I was in a marriage that was enduring only because of the nagging guilt and responsibility that I felt for Seb. My teenage inability to make a decision that would have been right for us both weighed heavily on me for many years, and I longed for some headspace. And so, with very little thought and emotions running at an all-time high I decided to rent a house, and rather foolishly we decided to live together.

And immediately it became very apparent that something was very wrong. He would be fine one minute and then his mood would change, for no logical or apparent reason. This would happen completely out of the blue and his reaction would be disproportionate to reality. There was no logical explanation and was very much a classic "Jeckell and Hyde" scenario.

I felt as if I was in the moving floor section of a Fun House, not knowing from one minute to the next when I was going to be thrown off balance. I knew that it was some sort of disorder but did not have a clue as to what. I could not believe the intensity of the situation and was absolutely pole axed by what I was witnessing. I would be perceived to be the kindest person in the world, to the most disgusting, useless, and stupid lowlife who had ever walked on planet earth, from hero to zero in a nano second.

For every few days calm, there would be an episode and I would become the world's worst person again and he would rage. The language and name calling during an episode was without question extremely abusive and I was terribly shocked. Dad's rages were off the Richter scale at times, he physically used to look like a completely different person, and I was very scared in all honesty during a few of them. His views were very polarized either black or white with no grey area or middle ground. There was absolutely no reasoning at all with him whilst he was having an episode, and it was like trying to have a productive conversation with a two-year-old child having a full-on temper tantrum. He would also use all or nothing statements when talking about me or situations that he had experienced such as; always, never, good, bad. If I challenged anything illogical, he said, I was met with responses that could only be described as word soup which concerned me. But there was an incredibly kind side to him, and this perplexed me. He was more akin to a wounded animal, than someone who sought out and consciously preyed on others for fun. I felt rendered inert by the whole situation and in hindsight the rages I was witnessing had put me into a state of shock.

In between the rages and when he was calm, he would often do the most thoughtful of things. One afternoon our collie was in the garden, and I noticed a baby rabbit was sitting under a bush. Unfortunately, Princess had clocked it too and went running towards it at a rate of knots. I called her to come back into the house and luckily, she did. But I noticed that the rabbit had collapsed, and I couldn't bear to have a look incase it had died. And so, I called dad to pick it up and check on it for me. I went back in the kitchen to make tea, and he came back about ten minutes later. And told me it was absolutely fine; he had checked the entire garden, and it must have run off. I went outside to check and much to my relief it had gone and thought no more of it. Dad admitted a few weeks later that it had died, probably of fear because it was so tiny, and he had buried it quickly in a tin in the flower bed.

It took me sixteen long years to find out what was wrong, and I did so purely by chance. I was looking at a site which was not focusing on any particular disorder but had some comments about something called BPD. A lady had posted on the site and described in detail what her son did during a rage. How he looked and what he said, and it was precisely the same as dad. Finally, I had an answer, and I began to research all that I could to understand this terrible disorder.

There are four sub-types of BPD: discouraged, impulsive, petulant and self-destructive. Dad without a shadow of a doubt falls under the sub-type of having Petulant BPD. He fluctuates between outbursts of explosive anger to feelings of being unworthy or unloved.

The disorders name does not help, as it almost implies that the sufferer is on the borderline or cusp of having a personality disorder which could not be further from the truth. Recently there was a piece written in one of the main newspapers regarding Zoraya Ter Beek and her choice of euthanasia, to release her from her struggles with BPD, autism and depression. The article stated she had a borderline personality disorder, as if it was one of many. Why write a piece without actually researching what it was? On reading her story it concerned me that euthanasia is being permitted for disorders such as BPD. The reason being is because as a rule sufferers' moods are so unstable and, in the moment, what if she feels differently on the actual day?

I can normally cope well with all factors of his BPD the depression, the disassociation, and the periods when he behaves recklessly. However, I confess to struggling with the hero to zero phase. Which only a mental health professional or someone that lives with a BPD sufferer will completely understand which is called idealization, discard and devalue. This behaviour is directed usually towards the person that has been allocated the role of "favourite person", a role that is impossible to live up to.

There have been MRI scans of people with BPD which have shown that three parts of the brain were either smaller than expected or they had unusual levels of activity.

- The amygdala plays an important role in regulating emotions, especially the more negative emotions such as fear, aggression and anxiety.

- The hippocampus which helps regulate behaviour and self-control

- The orbital frontal cortex which is involved in planning and decision making.

The development of these parts of the brain is affected by your early upbringing. These parts of the brain are also responsible for mood regulation. A number of environmental factors seem to be common and widespread amongst people with BPD. These include:

- Being a victim of emotional, physical or sexual abuse

- Being exposed to long term fear or distress as a child

- Being neglected by one or both parents

- Growing up with another family member who has a serious mental health condition.

Dads' childhood was pretty much the norm for a working-class family in the 1940's. Both his parents worked long hours though and he described himself as a latch key kid. He loved his mum a great deal but there were issues between him and his father. Who apparently favoured his older brother and was vocal about his preference which hurt dad a great deal. He told me also that whilst he was living at home his father didn't speak to him for several years, which must have affected him terribly. His father was apparently a very quiet man who came from a very large family. His paternal grandfather was a docker and an alcoholic who used to regularly beat his wife up in front of the children. Whether this affected his father and this filtered through to his parenting skills and his relationship with dad I have no clue, but I feel there is a clear connection.

When he is in a good and rational head space, he is very candid and freely admits to experiencing all the feelings and behaviour related to BPD. The one criterion that does not apply to him is actually self-harming although he regularly talks about suicide. He calls the episodes either Berserker Syndrome or having a Riastrad. Which is a "process by which a warrior physically morphs into a savage animal prior to battle". He will identify with anything that he considers to be normal alpha male behaviour, rather than to fully commit to accepting that he has a problem. Because of his lack of self-identity his persona can literally change overnight, and sadly an awareness conversation is completely forgotten the next day.

He often speaks about an actor called George Sanders who committed suicide after a series of tragic events and serious health issues. Although he has not dealt with the same traumas, dad identifies with him and with one of the suicide notes found near him: "Dear World, I am leaving because I am bored. I feel I have lived long enough. I am leaving you with your worries in this sweet cesspool. Good Luck". I hope that I never see those words written by his hand.

I have read a great deal about BPD, one book which was particularly helpful was "Stop Walking on Eggshells" by Paul T Mason and Randi Kregrer it is an excellent read. The book taught me many things one of which was during an episode to mentally take a step back and remind myself that his uncontrolled emotions are simply being projected onto me, as a release valve and are not a personal attack, it is merely someone acting out their pain. I implemented all the books recommendations, some of which I had to practice until they became second nature. There are many sites on YouTube that are helpful one in particular is Dr Daniel Fox who is an expert on personality disorders, he speaks from a stance of compassion and explains the whole dynamic extremely well.

Anything can set off an episode and often I am unaware of what has been the trigger. It might have been something he has been thinking about for days and then the slightest thing tips him over the edge. But there are a few particular things that I know are triggers...

- Any added external pressure or stress
- Any deviation from his daily routine without prior warning
- Perceived rudeness
- Changes in environment even something small like changing the colour of a towel
- Boredom can lead to him inciting a drama to alleviate the state
- Strong smells such as paint
- Too much talking will stress him out and when calm he tells me that the words all sound jumbled, and it confuses him
- Physical Pain

It is incredibly difficult after a particularly bad episode to implement empathy and understanding, but I dig deep and usually manage to do so. I pray for him and ask God what I should do. And the answer is always the same shine far brighter than the disorder, be calm and compassionate, it is not his fault he knows not what he does. And in all honesty, when I implement these wise words, they always work. When the episode eventually passes, he will say "I don't know why you bother with me, I am not worth the effort". One reason is, if I felt so alone, petrified and confused that I pushed everyone away. Would I still want someone to try and reach through my pain and make me feel loved, if even for the briefest of moments? Yes, I would.

For anyone who lives with a loved one with this disorder here are a few tips that have helped me cope.

Make sure you get enough sleep, as when you live in a highly reactionary environment and are exhausted it is much harder to stay calm.

On good days it is all too easy to forget that your loved one has a disorder, always be aware that the disorder is ever present. As it is less of a shock to the system when the next episode occurs.

It is all too easy to neglect your physical and mental health when living with someone who has this disorder. Take some B vitamins and magnesium and have some "you time" whenever you are able to.

Do not Justify Argue Defend or Explain it does not work and just exacerbates the situation.

Have a world rant on sites like BPD family once in a while, it helps to know that you are not alone.

Dad lives in whatever moment he is currently feeling. Happy moments and memories are remembered but the feelings they invoke are not retained so he can never draw on them to give him comfort or to self soothe. Subsequently he has no gauge or reference point as to how a person has behaved in the long term. His thoughts are instant, and his reactions are based on these immediate thoughts, whether they are based on facts or they are illogical it has no relevance.

Although the disorder and the person are a package deal there is a grey area, and all of us are far more than a label. And I appreciate dads positive character traits, he is incredibly deep and is knowledgeable with regards to world issues and historical events, and we have many interesting discussions about life and the world. He also has without fail had my back and is protective of his loved ones on a very practical level. Sadly, with regards to interpersonal empathy, he has difficulty showing it. However, if he watches a sad film, he can readily cry and feels tremendous sadness which is genuine and very deeply rooted.

However, although he struggles tremendously with what to do and say when someone is upset, he was quietly supportive and listened to me when I went no contact with my mum and the aftermath. Both he and my daughter stood by me and remained firmly in my corner, and I am eternally grateful to them both.

As I have the ability to self-reflect, I know why I have reacted the way I have and tolerated behaviour that others wouldn't. Some of the reasons are related to psychological fleas which I used in the past to protect myself, others are simply rooted in empathy and understanding and also my faith comes firmly into the equation. All of these enable me to understand to a lesser degree just how overwhelmed he becomes and to also turn the other cheek. Do I love my dad? yes of course I do. Do I think BPD is one of the cruellest disorders for the sufferer and also their loved ones? That's a big fat yes from me.

I believe the power of prayer with regards to mental illness is incredibly important. We are in troubling times and I can fully understand why many people are not coping. Prayer has helped me and although he does not know it or recognize it, dad has benefited from my prayers. If you are in the same boat, honestly give it a go, I think you will be surprised.

So, both my parents have a Cluster B disorder which is a bit of a shocker and not what I expected. Perhaps some of you will be thinking my mothers behaviour was less damaging than my fathers. Not so, although I have been very hurt by his words, I know he has an extremely good heart but a troubled mind. I see a good spirit and soul that is confused and frightened some of the time. And he lashes out because he does not know how to act otherwise. What you see is very much what you get with dad, he is not remotely fake like so many people are in this crazy world. If dad says he will do something because he cares about you, he will do it and he would do it to the detriment of himself. His good side far outweighs his bad and that is what I hold on to when things are going pear shaped. I have taken the time to learn about this disorder and not to vilify him, because it is the worst thing you can possibly do and it does not help the situation.

Although there have been many terribly sad memories, luckily there have been far more special ones. One being, once whilst we were out in the car in early December. It was snowing heavily and had laid on the ground. Suddenly he took an unannounced sharp turn to the left and drove down a dirt track that was near the house that we lived. It was farmland and the road that the tractors used, the surrounding fields were undulating and beautiful. Although the roads were icy and uneven because there was no other traffic, I was not scared, and I thought it was funny. The snowflakes were the largest I had ever seen and glowed magically in the car's headlights. It was the most thoughtful thing to do, and I felt like an excited seven-year-old a week before Christmas. Who was on a sleigh which was on route to see Santa in his grotto. I turned to him with the biggest grin on my face and said, "Dad I am having a sleigh ride" he smiled back and said, "We most certainly are Kim".

Dad is eighty years old and is currently struggling tremendously with his age and also with what is happening in the world, which I completely understand. My dearest wish is that when he dies it will be peacefully on a day which has been calm and he is not too troubled. If only he reached out and had DBT it would have helped him extricate himself from his self-limiting bubble. I have seen all sides to him both the good and the bad, the happy and sad. He has pushed me away many times, but I have still reached out to him and when he thanks me for doing so, and I know that he means it.

Thanks Dad :)

Song/Music:

Cu Chulainn played by Davy Spillane

A Small Measure of Peace by Hans Zimmer

ROOM 20

All Things Must Pass

I received a notelet from my aunt informing me that her sister had lost a battle with breast cancer. My first reaction was what I can only describe as odd, I felt detached but extremely sad at the finality of the words. Within its brief contents she asked me whether I would let Ross know as she was not speaking to him. After he had said some "unforgivable" things to both her and her sister which had resulted in them going "No contact". She had absolutely no comprehension that I had not spoken to him for years. This highlighted the continued absence of healthy and honest communication within the family. I felt no relief, just sadness that mum had died in a way that I would not wish on anyone. I proceeded to write back to her sending my condolences and thanking her for telling me the news.

I was ok for about a week but awoke one morning feeling sad that mum had died and had probably been in pain. She had given birth to me and not put me up for adoption, she had knitted me a very pretty cardigan, and I loved the little Christmas house. And so, I brought a candle in a glass holder with her initial on it, and later that day I placed a white rose from my garden beside it. I lit the candle and I spoke to her as if she was in the room with me, I told her that I forgave her and

I wished her peace. I read Ecclesiastes 3:1-.8 and decided to play a few songs. One of which was Creedence Clearwater Revivals "Long as I can See the Light".

Because regardless of the past I wanted her not to be in a state of limbo because of her narcissism, but to go to heaven. When we all die, I have always believed that without exception we are replayed our "lifetimes" actions by an assigned angel. Any behaviour which has hurt another human being or was simply not acceptable is discussed with us. All misdemeanours' whether committed consciously or subconsciously are brought to our attention to enable us to self-reflect and improve. This will apply to my mum as well as every one of us, unless we are the perfect soul all of us will receive a gentle but firm talking to. I finished my private service off with a little singalong to Wonderful World by Louis Armstrong, not in my best deepest voice but my own. I know that I will cry many more times in my life, but my last tear was shed for my mum and the relationship that never was.

Song: Side by Travis

As for my concerns with regards to my half-brother Bob's involvement in the disclosure to Ross there is an update....

I finally took the bull by the horns and explained to dad that I needed to have closure with regards to the matter, and he understood. It was not at all healthy keeping this essentially to myself for over ten years. Although dad's relationship with his son is important to him my feelings had to come into the equation also. And so, when he next visited, whilst dad was present, I finally confronted another elephant that had squatted in the room.

I calmly brought up the subject of the SIM card and my other concerns. Which was his insistence that he downloaded some files for dad onto our computer and plugged his hard drive into our laptop. Shortly after he was in financial difficulty, and all my limited emergency savings were stolen from my bank account, in repeated withdrawals mostly payments to Jackpot Joy.

I am incredibly careful with my bank details and computers and the only time I had entered them was post "installation" into a well-known shopping site. After the theft I had a thorough spring clean of the computer and immediately on removal of "Dad's files" the computers imagery became far sharper, and its performance which had been running at a snail's pace returned to normal. I was certain that Bob had installed keystroke spyware.

So, all the above was raised, I was composed throughout and the only time I had a catch in my voice and had tears in my eyes was when I brought up what had happened with regards to the disclosure and Ross. His response was strange; firstly, he informed me that he was more than capable of using his computer skills for his own financial ends. However, if it had been him, he was so adept on the computer that he would never have been caught. He was edgy and his hands kept flexing and he went incredibly white. However, he spoke like it was not even touching the sides it was the oddest reaction I had ever seen.

With regards to the SIM card and the phone call to me regarding Ross texting him. He had absolutely no recollection of ever calling me. And completely avoided answering any of my questions and told me that he did not have any of my personal phone numbers. He also said he had no clue who Ross was and did not know anything about the situation with regards to my stepfather. Dad at this point interrupted him and told him that it was not so, as he had spoken to him about it. He responded with If it was the case, then what we were saying must be true and he had forgotten, because he has a terrible memory and he had always been mental!

Luckily dad remained incredibly calm throughout and said to him "Bob if you were in Kim's position what would you think, bearing in mind you constantly tell people about your computer skills, and you always have had an unhealthy interest in other people's lives?" He responded, "I would think precisely the same". The conversation gradually came to an end, and I didn't push my point, there was no need, I had finally said my piece.

If I had been accused of something I hadn't done, I would have openly defended my position with facts. I would have undoubtedly been passionate emotional and annoyed. He purveyed nothing verbally and all I could deduce from the conversation was that he didn't care and was responsible for some or all of the things that had happened.

Closure is so important and the only way it can truly be achieved is by evidence gathering and self-reflection. Knowledge is the key and utilizing what you have learnt or discovered is far better than floundering around in the dark clueless or burying your head in the sand. I have moved on and have processed a great deal of emotions. I remain unsure as to what role my mum played in the disclosure whether she instigated it, or Bob did I shall never know. But I suspect that they both played independent roles.

Jealousy, guilt and fear are the most destructive emotions and damage the soul. I have felt jealousy very fleetingly in my life, then I felt guilty that I was feeling this negative emotion. I have felt fearful at times often unnecessarily so and I have also felt guilt due to my own actions not being as they should have been. All these emotions can swallow you up if you let them take hold of you. Prayer and acknowledgement and repentance when it is called for, truly does clear the decks. It must be all consuming and a terrible cycle to be in when these emotions are self-perpetuating and never addressed.

I admit that I did struggle to forgive Bob because I felt that by me doing so, he would never be held accountable for his actions. Simply saying the words" I forgive" does not mean that the sentiment is true or comes from the heart, for words are often empty. I confessed to God that I was struggling and that I didn't forgive him. I could not hide this from God because he would have known. It takes time and effort and honesty in prayer but when the forgiveness penny finally does fall from heaven, your heart does become so much lighter. If we repent and God forgives us for all the terrible things we do, then we must try and do the same if at all possible. The penny eventually dropped but I will never put myself in a position in which he is able to hurt me again, because that would be incredibly foolish.

In an ideal world it would be wonderful if there could be a happy ending to this story and I could see both my younger half -brothers again. But there are other factors in the mix that affect healthy and honest communication. I know that the odds are stacked against us with regards to us having a productive conversation that would enable us to move past this. The only way that it would succeed would be if I down played or denied what happened to me and it is something that I cannot do. I have grieved for them, and although they are alive, I have had no option but to consider them dead. I often think about them, and they are always in my prayers and I sometimes have dreams in which I give them both the biggest of bear hugs.

Songs: All Things Must Pass by George Harrison

For my youngest brother Run by Leona Lewis

And for both of them Hey Brother by Avicii xxx

THE LIBRARY 21

A Shop, A Long Shot & A Helicopter!

Apparently when you have a "Calling" which involves others you will be met with a great deal of opposition and also disbelief. So, the human naysayers and doubters were out in force, and there was nothing I could do on that score. But there was also something else at play in the form of supernatural opposition. I have always affected electricity and computers and phones when an emotion becomes heightened or I am concentrating. And this computer had an absolute field day with regards to the planned word count, something very dodgy clearly was not a happy bunny. It was only because I am thorough and cross referenced constantly that I could keep on top of things. At times I placed my cross over the screen and would pray, and things would eventually settle down. Chapters would disappear on a running word count, and then an old unedited version would reappear in its place the next time I checked. I would download the very same version of the manuscript and each word count would be different, it was nuts.

After submitting a second round of submissions over a period of approximately eight months, I felt that the human opposition was far too great an obstacle. And I decided to write a lengthy introduction for my eyes only and have a single personal copy printed.

In the new Introduction, I wrote an analogy with regards to how the masses were fully aware of what was happening around the world and why one day we would win.

And Here Is Verbatim What I Wrote...

"The truth deck of cards must always be ready to be played, and the tired and overused dummy pack needs to be firmly placed back in the stained and shabby box. The cards edges are ragged through overuse and many of us can tell what the latest card is without needing to look at the front, it's face has no value anyway and is fake and duplicitous. The deck is rigged, and the dealer is not as sharp as he thinks, it's time for a reshuffle in every way possible, with each and every one of us taking our turn at dealing the new deck which contains their very personal bespoke real truth card too."

A few days later I went to a new charity shop on the outskirts of town. The shop was tiny but full to the brim with many items, some of which I recognized as collectables. There seemed to be far too many staff in such a tiny space, and they greeted me as I entered. It had a very warm and welcoming vibe, and I immediately noticed a sculpture of some praying hands behind the till, and I was unsure whether they were for sale. I spoke to the owner Wilson, a tall quiet man and explained that I loved anything ecclesiastical. And he replied that he did too, and that I could buy them for a tenner. I was extremely pleased with my purchase and decided to drop off some nice quality donations at the shop a couple of days later.

One of which was a pair of wooden book ends, they looked Chinese and had a chinoiserie vibe going on. And had been expertly hand painted with two different birds on either end. I went to the shop with the bookends and a pretty mirror and was greeted by Wilson. I handed him the donations and proceeded to look at the many items in his little shop. Whilst I was doing so, he suddenly piped up "These are very unusual they are hand painted have you ever considered they are a one off"? I hadn't in all honesty, even though I had looked for a pair similar on the internet but to no avail. We spoke a little more about the shop and life in general and just as I was about to leave, I noticed a little ornament. A group of three mice, whom I thought were having afternoon tea. As per usual I hadn't put my glasses on. I picked it up and asked Wilson how much it was, and he replied the princely sum of £2. I purchased it, thanked him and left for home. And after putting my food shopping away I turned to my new purchase.

And I couldn't believe my eyes, it was a replica of my card playing analogy in the form of three little mice. Sitting at the centre of the table was the dealer, he was holding several cards and also had laid more than his opponents. His body was turned to his right and he was concentrating solely on the male mouse. Who had a card positioned between the toes of his right foot. His leg was extended, and he was passing the card to a lady mouse, to the dealers left. It had a blue label on the table marked Saxony, and underneath it was impressed the number one. The item itself was not unique but its quality and the number one on its base did set it apart. I couldn't believe what I was seeing but I didn't like the representation of the dodgy evil mouse so, I put a tiny little blindfold on him to ensure that he would lose the rigged game.

Wilson had made a point in bringing my attention to the bookends, so I googled the spiritual significance of the birds on them which were a Red Cardinal and a Blue Jay. The result was "If you are fortunate enough to spot a Red Cardinal and a Blue Jay together it is said to be a sign of good luck. The story goes that these two birds are natural enemies, so when they're seen in the same place, it is a symbol of peace and harmony". It seemed that I was being guided to put my foot back on the pedal, and so once again I did.

But I knew because of the book's narrative and the fact that I had absolutely nothing in my favour with regards to the "crowd pull" factor, that I was flogging a dead horse. Admittedly at this point the book was absolutely awful, but I knew that the concept was good, and with a great deal of help it could have been transformed into a humble but very beautiful stallion. And so, I decided to think completely out of the box, and I did something that I would never normally do in a month of Sundays. I sold some items on Ebay and ordered twenty Doxdirect editions to send to GB News in July 2021. I was on precisely the same page as them, with regards to the importance of news channels not being biased. And there being equal representation and coverage from both sides of a political debate. I had stopped watching any news coverage in this Country because of this, and I like millions of others spent many wasted minutes shouting at the telly. Whilst the BBC and Channel 4 tried to force a particular narrative onto the nation, and would happily try and belittle any guests on their shows in any way possible.

Although highly improbable I thought perhaps one of them may know of a literary agent who would understand the concept and the importance of a book written by an ordinary person, who was not a celebrity. Over the next couple of months, I felt sure that at least four of them had read some or all of the book because...

Andrew Doyle whilst discussing The Edinburgh Festival and the amount of people crammed into a space, he referred to the conditions as a "Petri Dish". Which I suspect is not that unusual, but I had never heard anyone else use it as a simile before. And then Nana echoed part of my equality rant in which I had used shouty capitals and had written "WE ARE ALL THE SAME". Also, I had rather naughtily used the word bollocks a couple of times in the same chapter and Mark used the word several times. And finally, Colin was talking about the shortage of truck drivers and said something like " I don't want to sound like a Pollyanna but..." Even though they couldn't help me I was sure that it was their way of acknowledging my very amateurish but passionate effort, which was incredibly kind of them.

Whilst trying to do what I could with regards to the book, life carried on as usual. And if I went past a local charity shop I would either leave a donation or buy something that I liked or needed on the cheap. And a few months later I brought Wilson a few more items. One was a Sylvac terrier dog ornament which someone had painted a glossy black, a red collar had been added and they had also inserted two twinkly blue gems for eyes. It was bespoke and unique. A few weeks later I went back to his shop and low and behold the dog had been put into a container and was sitting on a wooden chair which was surrounded by Quality Street with a sign next to it which said "This Dog Gives Away Sweets". It was lovely that the little dog I had donated was on the counter, and I felt a personal connection with the shop. A couple of months later I purchased an onyx bear from my favourite car boot, which had the very same twinkly blue gems for eyes. And although I had it out on display for a while in my home, I knew that one day I would give it to Wilson, when the time felt right.

My daily life carried on as usual, but unbeknownst to me I was soon to have the biggest shock of my life.

At around 8 pm one evening dad was upstairs in the back bedroom watching television with headphones on, with our new rescue dog Pickle. Whilst I was downstairs sitting quietly and thinking about the world and the damage that Covid had caused. I thought about the evil behind it and of all the negativity and terrible cruelty which was currently surrounding our planet. I had watched a mass prayer in Brazil on YouTube which was on an extremely long road. The camera panned along it and the hundreds of people who were praying. It was beautiful and a display of unity, but it saddened me. As although in prayer the pain and suffering was etched onto the majority of people's faces, and I felt what I can only describe as impotent. I cried for them and all of the people in the world who were also suffering. I prayed with every ounce of my being for good to overcome evil and for light to shine in the darkest of places, joy to replace sadness and did so for about twenty minutes. Although I knew good would eventually prevail, it seemed like evil was currently winning this battle, and I felt pretty peeved about it.

I rebuked all that was evil and did something that I had never done before and won't do again. I said to "he who must not be named" that he may be currently fooling many people and believe that he had got a firm hold on the world, but he hadn't. God would soon have the very last word and he would be defeated, and I was not in the least bit afraid of him... Which as it happens wasn't the wisest of things to say and was of course untrue.

Just as I have had a lifetime aversion to fortune tellers and tarot card readers. As a child if someone mentioned the "dreaded name" in any of its forms. I would tell them it upset me and not to ever say the words near me again. So, it was officially on my fear factor list, along with maggots' anaesthetics and a very odd one, helicopters. I don't like the roaring sound the blades make on take-off, how quickly they manoeuvre, how low they can fly, and how people can alight from them mid-flight. I have always found them invasive and incredibly creepy.

Suddenly my blood ran cold, and a sense of dread ran completely through my body. Although the lights were on in the living room they dimmed, and the room felt odd and other worldly. I felt alone and afraid and as if I was the only person on the planet. And suddenly from above I heard the loudest of noises, it was the whirring of a helicopter's blades. I wondered why on a winters evening would a helicopter be flying directly above the house without landing, surely it would crash. The noise of the whirring blades got louder and louder, it was deafening, and I wanted to run outside. My reasoning being that if I stepped outside other human beings would see me and then this unrequested supernatural bubble would burst.

However, on looking outside at the houses to our rear the wind generated from the blades was incredibly intense. The TV aerials were swaying and bending as if they were in the eye of a storm. No way was I going out there, and I knew at that moment I had incited something extremely unpleasant, and they had a massive beef with me. I truly thought I was going to die and envisaged dad finding me in a heap on the floor and presuming that I had died of a heart attack. I had nowhere to run to, and automatically felt it better and safer to be at ground level and laid out face down, prostate on the floor with my arms out to either side. I was more than certainly a goner and said to God. "If I am to die because of the evil that has found me and is surrounding me, please pick me up and hold me in your arms and never let me go. I love you Lord I am not afraid, please forgive me for all my earthly sins". With my eyes remaining tightly shut I waited barely breathing for the arrival of the dreaded "Voldemort". And then the deafening noise stopped, and the room was precisely as it was before. I pulled myself up and sat bewildered on the floor, the tears flowed, and I repeatedly said, "Thank you Lord". I felt humbled to such an extent that it is truly impossible to express or to ever adequately put into words.

Dad had not heard a thing, and it would not have been wise to relay this hum dinger of a crazy experience to him. But when he came downstairs for a cuppa, he knew that something was wrong and asked me if I was OK. I replied that something had upset me, and asked him if he could stay downstairs with me for the remainder of the evening, which he did thank goodness.

I subtly asked a few of my neighbours the next time we spoke whether they had recently seen a helicopter hover very low over our houses and none had. It didn't make me doubt what had happened, it just confirmed that it was a supernatural event that only I had experienced. The experience left me in absolutely no doubt that God is beyond powerful, and he showed me just how mighty he is. And when the time comes for the ultimate and final spiritual battle whatever cruelty his opponent uses or deploys it has absolutely no chance, all will be ok. Although I remain aware of Voldemort, I am no longer fearful. I wondered why the helicopter was part of the experience and thought perhaps it was simply because it played directly into my fears, and more than likely it was. But I googled helicopters and the bible, and I was shocked to discover a potential link to the book of Revelation. If in the very unlikely event there is a connection. My take on my experience is that either I had goaded the bad and was rescued by the good. Or I was being tested to see whether I would declare my full commitment to God in the face of death.

A few months later I found the strangest little drawing which I had done when I was about six and talk about freaky. I can remember making a particular part of it out of tin foil and I had spent ages trying to form it into the correct shape. It was a depiction of two houses and Father Christmas is on a sleigh above one house with his reindeers. Only two were drawn as I struggled with drawing animals so I decided that they would have human faces instead with antlers. Not nice and they looked like something out of the latest Hannibal Lecter series. Above the other house there is a bolt of lightning made from tin foil and the house looks like it is under siege. I know some will say that it was because I had a bad childhood, it represented my inner most feelings and my fear of being at home. It was not the case, my drawings were the reverse because I wanted happy and sunny, I drew and painted what I yearned for. I felt that somehow the little girl who sat there drawing the card all those years ago foresaw what was going to happen one day to her adult self.

Throughout my life I have often been made to feel that I was not good enough. Even when I have excelled at something, it was often never commented on. Or my input has often been taken as an automatic God given, without so much as a thank you. I could not comprehend why I had been asked to write this book with no earthly back up. I needed someone to support me, who was prepared to bellow out to the world, "Yes, she is telling you the truth, get on board with her and help". I felt like I was in an internal battle and the self-doubting enemy inside me was holding me back. But by coming to my rescue God and his angels showed me that I was special in his eyes, and I was good enough to write 77777 words for him. And although this ego driven world has many favourites, God loves us all equally. It was confirmation that he had asked me to do this task, and that somehow or other I would eventually complete my mission.

The experience was an awful lot to get my head around and I did not tell a soul. Because I would be deemed an absolute basket case, I felt isolated from the world and most of the people around me. Who although I love dearly are not on the same spiritual page as me. Subsequently I was very reflective and felt a little tearful for several weeks after. One day I went shopping to my favourite market and spoke to my friend Harrison who sells jewellery and antiques, and like me does not go to church. We spoke about the world and the spiritual battle that was intensifying and tears welled up in my eyes. He asked me what was wrong, and I told him I was tired of seeing supernatural signs which I had to keep to myself. He told me that I must not worry, I was far from alone and that he had seen many too, and that it was all going to be ok.

I agonized as to whether I should put my helicopter experience in this book, as I know that it sounds absolutely crazy. I have told a few people I know about it, and with the exception of one person, they have believed me. Yes, they don't understand it, but one immediately told me that it was clearly a one-off test that I had been set. A lovely married couple also told me about a book which they had read in which there were similar "out there" stories told by professionals such as police officers, armed forces personnel and emergency workers.

Many more months elapsed and then something unexpected happened. After dad had a particularly bad episode, I did something that I had not done before, I went and stayed in a local B&B for a weekend. My room although very comfortable was incredibly hot, and I decided to wander around the town, trying to kill some time. I looked towards the local church which I had always felt drawn to, but had never set foot in. I walked up to it, thinking that the morning service would be over and decided that I would go in and reflect and pray. I hesitated at the door and saw that the service had not yet finished, but I decided to go in and sit at the back. And wow the church was one of the most beautiful I had ever been in, and it was a comfort to be around people who also believed and I decided to attend for a while. On the morning of the third service, I went to the beach and prayed my usual prayers but also asked God to give me an answer with regards to the book. I had exhausted every single possible avenue to get it out there and had no clue what else I was supposed to do.

I attended the service with my friend and afterwards, we decided to have a MacDonalds, but it was full and there were no free seats. And so, we decided to go to a local garden centre instead. But my friend took a wrong turn and we thought we would go to the local beach and try out a new cafe. We found one we liked and in it was a lady who had spoken at a previous service. I knew that it was an answer to my morning prayer. I told her about the book, but I knew that the words would not be written by me but by the church's congregation. It would be their stories of faith which would also have a song listed at the end of their personal message. She told me that the person I needed to talk to was a lady called Anna who had done something similar a couple of years ago.

And so, I did, and I immediately felt a strong spiritual connection with Anna, who is the sweetest of souls. I put an information pack together to show how the Amazon KDP process worked. Also, how the stories could be gathered in the easiest way possible, and finally how it could be marketed to reach out to as many people as possible. With the view to give any proceeds to charity. Its aim would be to show the world that although our beliefs may be the same, there is far more to each individual Christian than a stereotypical label or presumption. Whether it is something they do in the future or not, I am just glad that I passed the message on.

As for me I know now that my main church will always be outdoors. We are all different and neither location is right or wrong. As the eternal introvert I have a closer and more personal connection with God when I am alone with my thoughts and prayers without any distractions.

After I had passed on the literary baton, I felt that it was the right time to hand over the twinkly eyed onyx bear to Wilson. I wanted to thank him for selling me the praying hands and the little mice. On entering the shop, I handed him the bear and explained the relevance of it and its connection to the sweet giving terrier. I also explained that my nickname as a child was Mishka and why I had been called it. I told him that the bear was not a donation but a personal gift, which I hoped would bring him luck. I also told him about this book and that he was in it, with regards to the items that I had purchased, and that I had written very positively about him, but I had not identified him or his shop. Before I left, he introduced me to his new very handsome and extremely friendly dog Mojo.

Two weeks later I popped back in and Wilson told me that the bear had very quickly brought him luck. Twenty minutes after I had given it to him a customer had brought in a donation. Sadly, her mother had recently passed away and had loved what Wilson was doing and his shop. And she had requested that her daughter do a whip round from all her friends and family, and they had raised about £150.

At the time I was mulling over a problem which I had encountered and I was unsure as to what to do about it. And then suddenly he told me he wanted to tell me a story, which I listened to. And I could not believe my ears as it directly related to my problem. He had given me the answer that I had been searching for without even knowing the question. I thanked him and left the shop, and decided to return a week later.

And I gave him a copy of my latest book so that he could see what I had written, and to check that he was ok with it. And much to my surprise he told me that he had also written a book which was about his dog and his work as a detective. He showed me some of the book's inner photos on his phone and told me some of the books story lines. It was clear that he was incredibly talented both with regards to the written word and also artistically. All his Facebook followers had loved the snippets of his book which he had posted online. I told him about Amazon and what he could do to get it self-published to reach out to a wider audience if he chose to.

I knew that when I went into the shop the very first time that it was somehow meant. And the reason has gradually been revealed to me. It is as if everything has come full circle and all is finally settling down as it should be. I hope that Wilson has all the success he deserves with his book, and he continues to help all the local community's pooches and their owners.

Over the past year or so I have touched base with several people who are on the same page as me. And they have also experienced signs that have comforted them or shown them their place in the grander scheme of things. Like me they know that we are merely bit part players in a very big drama that essentially, we have absolutely no control over. All we can do is be kind to one another and pray if we believe in God.

I believe that millions of us have a calling and sometimes we do not know how to achieve our goals. I liken it to a mass of butterflies that are flying round a buddleia bush. We fly past each other and make connections that resonate with us on a subconscious level, but are not fully understood by either party. This process continues, and we meet up with others who are on the same flight path. And when we have all hooked up, we are then gently guided to land on the same flower head. And then we are finally shown the full picture.

Songs: Get Ready for It by Take That

For my lovely daughter "Bill" who loves David Bowie Starman

And for Erika I'm Alive by Celine Dion

ROOM 22

Please Take a Pew on My Cobalt Chair

As we are at the end of our journey together, I want to say thank you for listening to me as far too often like you I have been ignored. I am sure that there have been a few rooms which you have enjoyed passing through, and you enjoyed my choice of music. Whilst others that you couldn't wait to leave, and you wished that you had been issued a pair of ear plugs. However, you have shown strength of character and persistence qualities that set you apart from others, which is why we have got on so well and I shall miss you all.

A quote from the German philosopher Friedrich Nietzsche states "That which does not kill us, makes us stronger." and it is so very true. Like you I have had some injustices in my life, no more than most but I have always told the truth and been dignified in my actions, and yes, I have lost sometimes. But if I had to go through the same scenarios again and still lose, I would conduct myself no differently. I have cried many a tear, laughed like a drain fought against personal injustice and put my head often above the parapet. Regardless I will never follow the herd and will continue to pop my head up if I feel that I need to. I am here for such a short amount of time; and I am an individual and not part of a generic collection of thoughts and ideas. Sometimes I am in the majority and other times I am well out on a limb. My spirit must continually develop and if it involves me having more of life's dilemmas to address I would rather that than be spiritually static. When I see something beautiful in nature or someone shows me a kindness, I truly feel a joy that makes me almost burst with happiness, I am able to feel that because I have felt tremendous sadness. I would not change a single thing I am moving forward as I should, and completely connected to my aging reflection when I look at myself in the mirror.

I may seem a mass of contradictions believing in God, angels, and an ethereal realm but very much in the world I am living in. I am opinionated but proud to be so, that is what we were given a voice and a brain for. Ultimately, I believe that the only one anyone of us is answerable to is God, as long as you are accountable for your actions and your thoughts and mean well to others it's all any of us can do.

However long it takes the journey to true self-acceptance is worth every single step, we are all incredibly unique and special never ever forget it. Remember "the herd" whether a family unit, or a trusted institution may not always be right, by association, default, or not so subtle persuasion. Many herds have an egotistical arrogant or toxic dynamic, you must trust your own gut instinct and not what is being forced upon you. Those who constantly push a particular narrative usually have a personal or hidden agenda. Truth has common denominators that people can recognise and relate to, this encourages empathetic thinking which can lead to positive change.

Daily I hear people discuss many of the topics I have raised and like me they feel voiceless in a world which is becoming madder by the minute. Many have given up saying anything and have adopted a "let them all get on with it" mindset. It is easy to feel brow beaten but whilst we are still able to speak out, we must.

Song: Your The Voice by John Farnham

My aim when I wrote this tour guide was not a singular one firstly it was to try and change some people's perspectives with regards to Christians. I wanted you to know just how diverse we all are and there is no such thing as an atypical Christian. I hoped by opening up to you that some of you who are currently sitting on the spiritual fence, would possibly think about coming down on my side. But whatever your beliefs are, whether you are an atheist or an agnostic it is what is in your heart that counts. I like and love people from both these groups because they are good, kind and loving people. We accept each other for who we are and not because of a generic label that defines us. There is always middle-ground in the relationship dynamic and we do agree on many important things.

Secondly and it is connected with the above, stereotyping is an underpin of many of the world's problems. I wanted to use my relatable life story and my unusual character traits to challenge those who routinely stereotype others, for whatever reason. There is no place for black and white thinking and no group or person has the right to collectively judge others and make sweeping generalizations. Stereotyping is currently being used as a weapon, and I am tired of it. Being bullied as a child is bad enough, but now because of social media it is happening to people of all ages for all manner of reasons.

And thirdly by using my life experiences and the very fact that I am actually in two minority groups it was a snatch back of the overly and often misused victim card. Many atrocious acts of violence, terrorism, rape, murder and modern-day slavery affect millions of adults and children and how they get over their ordeals if ever, is a testament to the most incredible inner strength. True victims' lives are ruined and it's so terribly sad, the ones that overcome their pain are true survivors.

Song: Thank You by Alanis Morrisette

I wanted to also encourage all of you who have gone through similar life experiences and give you a virtual hug. This very simplistic itinerary was always a concept, and my dearest INFJ wish is that it is discussed and does bring about positive change. I am fully aware that it is not going to be considered well written within literary circles, but it never was about perfection, it was aimed for real people just like you. If we are singing from the same song sheet please pass these words on so our message is finally heard and is no longer a whimper.

Recently I wrote my final wishes regarding what I would like for my small final send off, for my daughter and or dad to action. In my what to do in the event of my death section, I have written "If you could look in my phone and anyone who has a smiley face next to their number, please let them know that I have kicked the bucket. Although you may not be listed in my phone as a contact we have connected and spent some precious time together. I cannot ring you and you will never know my name, but I am sending my virtual smiley face to all of you who accompanied me on our paradoxical tour. Stay strong and be true to yourself and I promise that you will not go far wrong.

IF

If you can keep your head when all about you

Are losing theirs and blaming it on you

If you can trust yourself when all men doubt you

But make allowance for their doubting too

If you can wait and not be tired by waiting

Or being lied about, don't deal in lies

Or being hated, don't give way to hating

And yet don't look too good nor talk to wise

If you can dream and not make dreams your master

If you can think and not make thoughts your aim.

If you can meet with triumph and disaster

And treat those two imposters just the same

If you can bear to hear the truth that you have spoken

Twisted by knaves to make a trap for fools

Or watch the things you gave your life to broken

And stoop and build 'em up with worn out tools

If you can make one heap of all your winnings

And lose it on one turn of pitch -and- toss

And lose and start again at your beginnings

And never breathe a word about your loss

If you can force your heart and nerve and sinew

To serve your turn long after they have gone

And so, hold on when there is nothing in you except the will

Which says to them "Hold On"

If you can talk with crowds and keep your virtue

Or walk with Kings nor lose the common touch

If neither foes nor loving friends can hurt, you

If all men count with you, but none too much

If you can fill the unforgiving minute with sixty seconds worth of distance run.

Yours is the earth and everything that's in it

And .... which is more....

You'll be a man my son. (forget the gender part it applies to ALL of us)

By Rudyard Kipling

I know you expected a real stained-glass window, in this room but it was a little too expensive. But I am as chuffed as a carrot with my hand painted glass jam jars and glass vases on the windowsill. The butterflies, flowers, hearts, and abstract angels were all pretty easy to do. But I decided not to attempt to paint Jesus as I wouldn't have done him justice, and I don't need to because he is in my heart.

And of course, I reached my intended word count of *77,777. And just as I planned to have that number of words in my secret contract. I knew from the get-go that the wonderful self-acceptance anthem by Chesney Hawkes "The One and Only" had to be in the book. I never really looked at the video because I was normally far too busy belting out the song. But whilst I was planning our tour, I thought I would give myself a wee positivity hit and looked at the video. And blow me down I could not believe what I saw......

I told you that signs can appear in songs video's.

Enjoy Your Room :)

* ALL THE INNER PAGES BUT DOES NOT INCLUDE THE COPYRIGHT PAGE OR LAST PAGE PRINTED BY AMAZON

THANK YOU

Thank you to all you musicians and composers whose music and lyrics have soothed me when nothing else could, many more songs and artists than I could list in this book.

Thank you to all of the individuals who contribute in many different ways and provide information about mental health issues and disorders.

Thanks to all those that have written poetry, prayers, motivational speeches and books, when I felt alone your words have given me comfort and a source of mental escape.
.

Thank you to all my work colleagues and friends from the past, I will never forget the good times we spent together.

Thank you my newly acquired "brother" Harrison for putting my charm bracelet together it is absolutely beautiful, and for often reminding me I was not alone.

Thank you my dearest friends I am blessed to have quality over quantity and I consider you all as family

To all of my loved ones residing in the "Big Mans" beautiful and very large residence thank you for loving me, we will meet again but until then..

Thank You for being the most loyal and beautiful friends my Princess Pudding and My Little Pickle Baby and our new addition Little Fella.

Thank you to my dear daughter Faye and my dear old dad, my earthly constants who have always stood in my corner and mean the absolute world to me, thank you from the bottom of my heart I love you very much.

Non-shouty capitals THANK YOU LORD for everything you have never deserted me, you have forgiven me and have always been my rock, fortress and confidant

I am proud and as chuffed as a carrot to be one of the 46% in the UK who firmly holds this belief. If you are in camp 54 it would be wonderful if just once and for me you could recite the following, simply because this world really does need a big old hug, and prayers are often answered when spoken in numbers.

THE FINAL HYMN

Praise To The Lord, The Almighty

&

THE VERY LAST WORDS

<u>The Unity Prayer</u>

Lord put an end to the shedding of innocent blood around the world.

Destroy the schemes of the wicked who monger after war and create conflict.

Quench the insatiable fire of the greedy and the murderous.

For these people will not inherit Your Kingdom and world to come.

Hear our heartfelt cry, Lord.

Amen

Printed in Great Britain
by Amazon